Selected Poems

1947–1967

Robin Skelton

McClelland and Stewart Limited 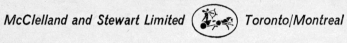 *Toronto/Montreal*

Selected Poems

1947–1967

Robin Skelton

Poetry by Robin Skelton

◦ ◦

Patmos and Other Poems (1955)

Third Day Lucky (1958)

Two Ballads of the Muse (1960)

Begging the Dialect (1960)

The Dark Window (1962)

A Valedictory Poem (1963)

An Irish Gathering (1964)

A Ballad of Billy Barker (1965)

◦ ◦

Copyright © 1968 by Robin Skelton

B69 25934

◦ ◦

Distributed in all parts of the world
except North America and Australia
by Oxford University Press, London

◦ ◦

The Canadian Publishers

McClelland and Stewart Limited

25 Hollinger Road, Toronto 16

◦ ◦

PRINTED AND BOUND IN ENGLAND BY
HAZELL WATSON AND VINEY LTD

contents

* * *

to

Sylvia,

Nicholas, Alison, and Eleanor Brigid

* * *

Preface

Although I began writing poetry as a very small boy, the earliest poem in my first collection was written in 1947 when I was twenty-two. I have therefore given 1947 as the year of my poetic beginnings for the purposes of this selection. I have chosen two other years as being equally significant. In 1957, I married and became a father for the first time. In 1962, I first set foot in Canada and determined to emigrate from England. Both these events fundamentally altered my way of life and my poetry; I have therefore divided this collection into three chronological sections, and added a fourth to include my ballads which seem to me to set themselves apart from the remainder of my work.

I have allotted the poems to their periods in accordance with their dates of composition, not their dates of publication, so that there are many poems first published in 1958 and later which appear in the section devoted to the period 1947–1957, and there are previously unpublished poems in the 1957–1962 section as well as in the 1962–1967 one.

The poems included have been chosen from five books and several pamphlets of verse published between 1955 and 1967. I have deliberately excluded from consideration my three longest poems and my translations from the French, Greek, and Gaelic, feeling that these would upset the balance of the collection. I have also omitted my poems about Ireland as these are inclined to be local in reference and specialized in appeal. In spite of these omissions, however, I believe that the present selection justly presents my main lines of development and the central concerns of my poetry over the years.

Prologue

1960–1962

On the Eve of All Hallows

Histories walk tonight;
clad in accomplished fate,
each takes his grievous turn;
candles in turnips burn
their spearblades on the dark
and quiver in the talk,
the after-silence. Here,
at the old end of the year,
I was born. My star
rose in this watchful mirror.

Now quiet is possessed
by necessary ghosts;
they too, born in between
the tide and the tugging moon,
found violence in the nerve,
had pity, suffered love,
and ached at beauty. Death
sighs on our common breath
and mirror. Ghosts, stand by
this poet of your family.

Poetry has been my line
from snivelling childhood on.
I have the usual scars,
the usual haunted face,
am lecherous enough;
I even have a cough,
though so far don't spit blood;
I plague my wife: it's said
Art is the one thing for
which everyone must suffer.

I stare down at the glass;
behind me my own face
encounters me; I turn
and parings twist my name;
my own words fill my ears;

what will survive? The stars
may tell in time, at least
will sieve away the worst
and probe with practised hand
the desolate remainder.

It is one thing to build
a poem and fix the world
around it, make it spin,
another to give stone
the lasting, bitten word.
Ghosts, listen. You have had
mortality's one proof;
I ask you for relief:
tell me these passions are
in more than the mind's mirror.

Some say poems have kept
a thought from being trapped
by staying on the move
like most wise beasts we have,
and some think them a mode
of clambering inside
the space between the fear
and the resultant prayer
of every man that wants
to last out the long moment.

I'd say mine were the lies
I had to fix in place
to keep Truth on the run,
for when the hunt is done,
the quarry faced, who knows,
as blood streams in the eyes,
what fingers grip? My hands
for purely mortal ends
tie knots which they untie
with difficulty, intently.

Nothing in me is fixed,
and nothing I have asked
comes from a firm desire;
I have no final prayer
tonight as my words all
turn ghosts within the still
and reckoning hour I face;
I claim no special grace,
for all my deaths are on
the point of being human.

I keep the mirror clean;
I watch it change, alone
with love of every nerve
of living that we have,
and see time unpick time.
I do not wear a name
except the end of speech.
The stars rock. And I reach
up from the drowning glass
my small necessities.

part one

the climb

1947–1957

Child

Tattered by light,
the child may see
deception in
an apple tree;

though singing birds
entrance the bough
his world is rocked
by here and now

till dark in bed
his moments come
to watch the other
side of sun,

as to his window
silent sky
swings a dreadful
finity.

The blowing wind
throughout his room
curls him smaller
in the gloom

till daylight come
to shred again
his apple tree
with leaf of pain.

◉

Man with a Guitar

In the small café where the lamps are caves
in the blue sad air, his halcyon gaze
broods on the waters where no man goes,

and the plucked salt strings of the drilling rain
pocking the slow swell have refrain:
this is the story that no man ends.

His fingers tuck from the blind guitar
the click of the shingle where no feet are,
the twang of the birds in the sea-washed tower

columnar and cold; in the wavery glass
the pillar echoes his melodies
ebbing away from the pebbled noise

of the tapping heels and the tumbling words
to a stillness of seas; his hands are birds
stirring within a cage of chords:

here is the music that no man ends.

◎

The Fence

Language, a peeling fence, cracks at the lean
of the silent creature we have always known
and patched with slats against, and nailed, and tied,
smelling through gaps the sweat that sours his hide,
and sometimes catching sight of hoof and horn.
They tell us wood is strong, that it has borne
his hard hurled shoulders from the very start,
though shaken still stands firm. Half-eased, we turn.
Behind us our own house is trampled down.

●

Advice from the Interior Self

Place the words round silence, so that form
indicates the centre, where all words
are without form and liquid as the spring
of living water, crystallized in roots
and buds and blossoms only where the wheel's
iron spinning rim that is the world
we must escape hurls round the central silence.

Place the words round meaning so their silence,
after teeth and tongue, contain the world
within its central stillness, round which wheel
the facts of language and the definite roots
and buds and blossoms that abuse our spring
with iron images, and let no words
lead outwards into accuracies, but form

them coronets about the void, where form
is absent, language stillness. Place your words
as you place breath, because from breath can spring
the life beyond the breath that has no roots
in lungs or altitudes. Our language wheels
about a stillness that escapes the world;
our words must move our meanings into silence.

◉

Heron

Stoop-shouldered heron, head awry,
stick-legged fisher in the stream,
stands alone as destiny;
we see him as we cross the fields,

a figure carved of reed and briar
native to the chill thin air
below the lock whose silver shoals
scatter through his agate stare

that sifts their nature, waiting for
the golden fin, the feathered tail,
of some irradiant star-crossed fish,
patiently as daylight fails,

and as we cross this lover's field
we see him standing grey and still,
and sudden through our shoal of talk
death's image arrows to the kill.

⊛

Flowers and Jar

The attitudes of flowers and trees are strange
bright irresponsibilities of earth;
their leaf and blossom emphasize that spring's
an alien language, far removed from love,
pain, or joy. Discover in the trees
the attitudes of green, but know them strange

to us and to our yearnings. In the spring
their gaiety is careless of the cold
bright steel of fear that threads our breath, and all
pain and joy of ours they do not know,
alien and apart. To think them kind
to us is lovers fallacy each spring.

Indifferent years change. We, held in them,
alien to their rhythms, think the jar,
bright on our table, may control, conceal
their perfidies, but jars, as flowers, leave love,
pain, and joy aside, are not our mould,
indifferent as flowers; we see in them

the attitudes of green, but know them strange.
Pain or joy discover in the trees
an alien language, far removed from love;
their leaf and blossom emphasize that spring's
bright irresponsibilities of earth,
the attitudes of flowers and trees, are strange.

⊛

The Toad

The crack in the rock split wide to our drill;
in a hollow round as a skull
was a still toad, held in unbreathing,
as if this cell
were sanctuary in the perpetual rock of grieving,

and we held back as dust on the blurred skin
spread its grey stain,
thinking the rock trapped him in his rainy leaping
to make this prison,
and held our hands to what was smally heaving

as if with the sudden sun-slap some living will
had been brightly spilled
into the stiff bulk, watched the blink and the fumbling
limbs that were limbs still
hop over the stone chips, roused to sky and stumbling,

and said, "When small he was held by the hollow stone,
but, tranced, lived on:
life locked from the start in its one little room
can still burn song,
hidden, have flame till what drill split the tomb?"

๏

The Cat

For Sam

The cat stood under the lilac.
It was black.
The sky was blue, the grass green,
and it stood
black under the lilac
that was lilac
under the sky that was all over blue.

No matter that the way we say is how
the thing is in the mind, a proof of sorts
that where we stand and look is what we are,
sometimes a black cat stands black under lilac
and the grass is green, the sky unknown.

◉

The Need

I want of mole and bird
their wise green and glad dark,
the felt mass of the seed
and the weight of rain,
and to huddle unheard
and small from dog and hawk
and know the wear of cloud
and clay next to my skin,

for earth and air are caught
blindly by nets of mind,
and lose all size weight space
in scales of miles and clocks,
until this frame of dust
grows meaningless in wind
though I would still rejoice
and mourn at noons and rocks,

and have each moment loud
unalterable kin
with running vein and breath
of valley cliff and moor
in which I learned to stride,
and through which I begin
to ask the face of death
what I am striding for.

◉

The Cotton Dress

Love in a cotton dress.
No steadfastness
of star or Philomel
or thorn-spurred rose
red in the darkness,
but this happiness
walking as simply
as shadows down the road
no symphony attends
or lurking Troy.
It would be moving
if not commonplace,
such casual mastery
letting them dismiss,
as we dare not,
the dark, the loneliness.

⁂

Theme

Theme of the altering stranger: in he comes,
ferns turned fronds huge as a hill, and words,
watching the ferns, grown loud as the slapped drums.
Theme of the questioner: we had not heard
that query of the clocks and curtains, and
no answer will come pat. What was that knock?
Apostle or postman, visitant or child?
Theme of the altering messenger: the look
askance from windows, hiding behind ferns
huge as the singing hills that watch and mock.

⁂

The Climb

For Michael Snow

Cramped on the rain-greaved steep of rock,
shouldering its grey weight, inching round
outcrop and nudge till skies are black
and brailling fingers, flake and crack
and footscrape taut to mock and trick,
sometimes there is no way down.

The lift of mind seduced us here
to make the pathless sheer a feat
significant in hope and fear,
but, pinned upon the need of near,
we hear the whisper at the ear.
Sometimes there is no retreat.

The straddled chimney, the shifting stone,
the slip and scatter of chuckled shock
into its echo, and the grown
demands of hands are ours alone
to tease us with the strength we own,
and always there is no way back.

◉

The Dark Encounter

For Geoffrey and Margaret Keynes

That day the barren island swooped like a gull
upon, then away from, the boat as we swore and pulled
through the rocks that were oily with sea-sweat
and warted with shells
to the blank shore crumpled with weathers
and hauled her over
the shingle and camped by the cliff in a midnight of squalls;

the next they left their forest, jostling, a herd
of sniffing and itching and clicking and staring hard,
and they shuffled up close to our boat side,
then, growing unawed,
they were daft loud laughter all over
and quick as fever
to mimic like mirrors our every gesture and word,

reflecting back our vision, learning to grope
in harshness for laughter, in grimace for smile or gape,
and at last we perceived there, distorted,
the dark of our scope,
and were bored black sick with the business
and started to curse.
We stayed there a week, exploring, but left without hope.

◉

The Slickensides

*"Slickensides" is a term used by geologists to
refer to stones which have been split by the
movement of the earth's crust in such a way as
to form two polished surfaces facing one another.*

"I sometimes think that stone," she said,
"the slickensides, is just like us,
lying lonely in the dark,
two surfaces as smooth as glass

reflecting darkness, every smile
of meaning missed, each nod or wink
locked in the dark reflective heart,"
and I replied, "I sometimes think

two mirrors in the barber's room
reflecting I and I and I
are caused by just such fracture of
the cosmic unity." Her eye

brightened then. "But *they* have light,"
she said. "The slickensides is blind.
You see yourself." I saw myself,
a name continually signed

upon the darkness or the light
reflectively, no foreign chink
intruding me. I said, "I'm blind. . . ."
And she replied, "I sometimes think. . . ."

◉

The Exploration

I walked into the mountain heart.
The corridors were choked with dirt,
the roof decaying. Rubbled stone
blocked the great gate of the room,
and the huge bones of animals,
long extinct, lay where they fell
below a gap of ragged light
becoming grey. It was too late
to pass the broken and the spilled
and venture on the room by night,
alone and sure that I would find
the dancing frescoes figured round
a central cold, a hollow place.
No man, alone, could lift his face
and stare upon them without dread
and understanding of the dead
shaking him until he bowed.
I turned back and my heart was loud
to hide from me in upper air
the secret running of the deer,
but all the walls of looming night
were figured with their wheeling bright
and breaking forms, and in each tread
I stumbled home those hunters bled,
those hunters dead. I could not sleep.
No images were mine to keep.
Man on his cross dies many times
and many times the mountains weep.

◉

The Horses

Dawn-bent Adam lifted his spade
for the seed of history; stiff as glass
the sky roofed time; the yellow sun
turned dull as gold, and on the grass
the horses paused and tasted air
as if they could foretell the dream
of wings and intellect, and soar
above the frozen attic scene
not yet in place: but Adam bowed
and reverently pressed down the clay
of that first rose; they tossed their heads
suddenly filled with strange dismay
and, caught by an unreasoning wind,
fled down the hill across the sands,
while dawn-bent Adam stood like stone,
looked at his scarred and earth-stained hands.

The Shore

For Kathleen Raine

Lanes of light lead down
to the deserted shore,
the empty standing tower.
Beside the fields of shells
the abstract dance of wind
is spinning scarves of sand
upon the patterning dunes
to phantom runes and spells.

The muted ocean lies
horizoned silver where
no boats will mesh the deep
and peopling swim of tide.
Within the tower the nets
hung salt-stiff on the wall
are sifting into sand,
the bleached door open wide.

So space before time was,
and here we find our end,
see down all lanes of light
this breath's perpetual place,
and in the tower our snares,
and in the fields of shells
our prayers, and in the sands
our dance of love or hate.

The abstract dance of wind
beside the open door,
the silvered ebb of sea,
remain as darkness folds
the visionary lanes
and we swing in the tide,
each knotted current loud,
each sea-deep dark and old.

◉

The Net

For Samuel Banks

The blue day was an apple in the hand
when she came smiling to his boyish wars;
the aeons were early and the gods were young.
No matter how you watch from where you stand
or if you doubt or symbolize the cause,
she smiled upon him and the smiles were young.

Time has no way of passing when we wake
such implications in the eyes and stance,
the blue day infinite in a grain of sand,
the fall impossible. We see them take
their places in the shaking breathless dance.
The aeons were early and the time was once.

But always lame and clever someone comes
and round the simple day the bright net falls.
They found their nakedness had been surprised.
She purified herself in Paphian foam
and he went cold and wise back to his wars.

◉

The Ball

Under the rock is an iron ball.
If you lie on your belly you'll see it there,
jammed between rock and rock at the top
of the roofed-in creek, so changed by air
and sea and age that its orange rust
burns like a sun. It is held fast where
rock roof meets rock. If you slither down
on a rope, he said, you can get quite near.

If you once get down, avoiding the pool
that is three foot deep, worn round by a stone
turning and turning upon the spool
of the spinning tide, and are big enough fool
to wedge your shoulders into that gap
you can touch the ball. It is rough with rust
and orange and ochre and red, he said,
a sun clamped down by a granite crust,

but you'll never move it. The sea is loud
as your heart as you lie on the slime and shift
your hand past your head as you chin the stone,
and every time that you try to lift
a muscle or twist the tide seems near
and the rock roof closer. The ball burns red
where roof meets rock: I hid it there
when I was a child of God, he said.

The Top

For Barbara Jump

Strain the cord round, tight as breeches
under the wall's lee, pull and curl
its staggering arc still, spun asleep
this city morning bright with rain;
so earth revolves; the leaf, now born,
now fallen, spins and is the same.

Fling wide arms out; sky-eyed as summer
in the hopscotch street, spin round until,
blurred as a top, the street is locked
in otherwhere, until the walls
slow into sickness; on their sides
the dead leaf and the top lie still.

And then again. The leaf, the top,
the body, spinning till their sleep
blurs time to that eternal poise
each prayer demands but cannot keep
one mortal morning. Wet with sun,
life, death, revolve and are the same

only at that point of rest.
We strain our cords, and pull, and lift
each staggering arc towards its sleep,
but cannot stay. Dream, deed, belief
slow into sickness, into time;
the world returns and is the same.

◉

King and Queen

For Henry Moore

The big hands idle on the robe-smooth stone,
the horned and beaked heads emptied by long pain
watch over the moors;
scooped thin with years,
the upright bodies keep their bench of bone.

Gently we come here, but do not kneel down;
hopelessly human dignity has outgrown
the formal reverence
and makes no pretence
to dominations stranger than our own,

who touch their sides and hands to have of them
solace, by emblem, of the wasting pain
in care found powerless
to protect or bless
children and kindred from the place of stone

in which we, too, obey dictates and crowns,
grown strangers to our own, so simply born
once to a girl
whose big hands held the world
and whose hard peasant knees pressed down the stone.

Third Day Lucky

Third day lucky,
he split the stone
with his thread of grass,
and shouting came
into his Easter,
the carved word split
open to sun
and the drilling rain,

announcing Adam
was man no more,
and the hole in the heart
a nest for doubt,
and the fish-thick sea
awake with praise,
and the figging branches
a-swing with fruit,

then climbed the stair
of the simple sun,
while time stood round
and time stood still.
Third day lucky,
we tell the tale
of Adam hanged
on a gallows hill,

and love nailed down,
and love come back,
and from the crack
in the temple stone
the new grass springs,
the dead word snapped,
blood on the jacket
of the bone.

⊛

The God

Feed the beast
that you weep for, having killed.
Garland the great bear
of the wood and hill.
Make him enter each house
with blessing snarl.

At his death rejoice,
eat all flesh up,
sing, send messages,
dance, feast, and weep.
The fathers have his ghost
whose blood you cup,

and hear his word.
The body bayed and torn,
worshipped and fattened,
that the village mourns
walks in darker woods
than stick and stone

drove him from in Spring.
His great frame hides
the hollow darkness
and the holy dead,
and his claws rage
where dynasties have died,

and on the post the skull,
unmasked, stares out
across the grain bowls,
arrows, spears, and nets,
protecting tribe and harvest,
long-fanged, white.

He has descended
the evil hill
across the black river
and the witchcraft trail,
carrying the lives that fed
and prayed and killed

to give the fathers
and tell all is well,
and in the sacred relic
of his skull
the dark gaps are
their oracle and will

who rule the country.
Animal and huge,
he was the hunting god
the body's rage
could recognize
and worship in his cage,

and weep and feast upon.
The seasons turn
stiffly upon
the dying and the born,
looking for him they killed
to come again

in the same shape
from the bestial Spring.
Evil spirits cower
from the song
wailing into the hills
of the journeying king

grunting along the trail
of blood and stone
into the fathers' forest.
The unknown
returns no message back
but the unknown,

and the seasons turn.
What pity have
the gathered centuries
across the grave
to send no more
than this for rage and love—

clumsy, rank, matt-haired,
with slavering jaws,
giant shoulders,
resinous black eyes,
yellow fangs,
rasped guttural of voice?

What meaning is there?
From the wooden bars
watching the white skull,
and with razor claws,
the new caught god
awaits our knives and prayers.

◉

At Tutankhamen's Tomb, Thinking of Yeats

I enter the tomb and remember
his chanted, laden words.
On fresco and papyrus gods
have the hooked heads of birds.
The flared dark echoes. The still golden
smile haunts and disturbs.

Artifice of a dead thing
mocks the hands that made,
the bestial tunnelling
into the mountain side,
and the inscribing eye
mastering lacquer and gold.

Broken complexities
of the meshed nerve and vein
shape coloured hieroglyphs
on wood and stone.
Past mire and fury phrase
peace on long bed and crown.

All that man is in his time
of laboured passion and need
is to accompany the journey
of the painted dead
whose toys and kingdoms rest,
is to guard the smiling head

skinned with gold. I remember
his senatorial voice
echoing the makers need
of a ghost's objective grace.
He built a golden bird
out of his raggedness,

and heard its clockwork sing
to emperor and queen
on Hades' bough of past
and passing and to come.
He had his thought worked out
and imagined on his tomb.

The single eye of Ra
looks cold upon his grave.
Horseman and hawk, the sun
swings by the bones that strove
huddled in dirt, or huddled
in their painted clothes.

Yet the long Pharaoh looks
with epicurean eyes,
firm in surfeit, content,
with life's epiphanies
gathered at head and foot
under the stones mock skies,

and I am kneeling down
in centuries and dirt
before a bandaged death,
the withered lung and heart
praising still, the small skull
still catafalqued in art.

Such sinews thonged and dried
rig every argonaut,
hang every fanatic oath,
and rock all bell-tongued weight;
umbilicus and cord
rope sands to keep us caught,

and that gilt smile the dark
conceals as torches burn
out in lifted hands
retains its living form,
and, passionate and gay,
its stillness will return

through time to what we made
when centuries beaten flat
above our journeying dead
are broken into dirt,
and years fall down like stones
before the reaching heart,

and, chronicled with lives
burned out to give us bread,
bound by the nerve and vein,
we lie untenanted
below the deserts waste
and know that we are dead.

For then that smile shines out,
as gods with heads of birds
and stick-legged scribes pretend
dead empery disturbs,
ghost journeys on in state.
His laden wrought-out words

leave as I leave the tomb,
this history ill begun
that must end in the dark
and passionate painted room
someone disturbs, disturbed, behind
his back the bird-beaked sun.

⊛

At the Cavern's Mouth : A Dialogue

For Alex and Pamela Currie

Once in the cave it was black as your hat.

No lights at all?

               I was blind with the shock.
I felt my way with nervous hands,
establishing contours of the wall—
humps big as hills, cracks deep as cracks
in the mind itself when a thing appals.

I carried a torch and the light came back
from the polished walls. I could see my way.

At first I was blind and for turning back.

But you didn't turn?

               I found the way.

It was easy, then?

It was pretty tough.
Though I got to see the different degrees
of shadow and dark, and the way the rough
hewn faces stared in the lighter bits
and the hanging bats, I was pretty scared.

But you found the place?

                    I found the place.

You were very moved?

                    It was black as your hat.
I rested a while and thought aloud
and sang to keep my spirits up.

You didn't see. . . .?

                    I didn't see
the crystal throne, the quartz like hands,
the coloured dome, the holy bone
fixed in the ice, or touch the bands
of silver round the central stone
they all report. I sat alone
in darkness there, and thought aloud,
and had a drink from the thermos top,
and heard the hollow echo as
I sang to keep my spirits up.

It was a failure then?

                    A flop.

You needed a torch. When I went down,
though I didn't go far, I could see it all;
the walls reflected back the light.

But you didn't go on?

                    I was sure I would fall
in a pit or crevasse and I'd left it late
so I came away.

                    You are going back?

Some day, some day when I have the time
and a guide as well.

                    You will go alone.
There are no guides, and the booklet says,
for some reason or other, that only one
is allowed at a time.

                    Was there much of a queue?

Not much. They mostly returned quite quick,
rather like kids who'd enjoyed the Wheel
tremendously, but looked rather sick;
they hadn't gone far.

                    You took no light.
That seems so odd when you knew it was black
and you'd have to grope your way by the side.

I took a light, but the battery died –
I'm happy to say.

                    Then it wasn't a flop?

It was failure alright, and that was the thing.
When you know you're blind and alone in the place
you think aloud and you start to sing,
and the echo tells you the hollow fact
that there is no image to tell the world,
no bright excuse for the easy air
of the travelled man.

                    But it's all been mapped –
photographed too!

                    When I was there
it was something else. I sat alone.
I'd found the failure and could go back.

An easy return?

                    I knew the way.

There seemed more light?

                    It was black as your hat.

   ®

part two

an uncertain meaning

1957–1962

Words in a Column

I, this ventriloquial pillar
in the wordy desert, throw back
in my maker's teeth the lingua franca
of a storm laughing under its breath.

Trajan added a column of dead
figures battling division by division
to the round gape of the arena, made
something to stand up to the gods' derision.

Not that it lasted. If you care to look,
the trusted heroics of a yellowed novel
strut with cracked voices, and the rock
words have elided into cant and rubble.

Ozymandias was in the same case.
Whoever it was that drew up Babylon
(and even the pyramids are flayed),
or sweated out that woman headed lion

(look at the painting scribbled off the wall),
believed the numen of the moment, lettered
carved and worded, would outlast
time and the wind, and could not be bettered.

Proof of a nothing proof against
nothing but indigenous self-grandeur,
a resolute emptiness derisive of
terrains and titles, cannon horse and armour,

what stands stands; in words or stone
the dead or alive outlaster
throws back into the brown teeth of the earth
a comprehension that is the true master.

And I, this ventriloquial column
set in my lettered ways, refract
what I reflect – the emptiness that rears
up its own monument made artefact,

not a triumphant arch, a giant verse,
but a storm laughing under its breath,
not at the futile pretence, but, quietly,
the need, the hesitation, and the choice.

        ◦ ◦

The Arrival

Listen. How long have you listened?
Have you been listening long?
I think I have been talking to you
ever since the world began.

Who are you who come to the door?
Who are you who walk up this step
where the grass is dry
and the stone is cold
and the winter a terrible thing?

Who are you who come from the sea
with hands of waves and eyes of storms?
Who are you who climb from the sea
with the song of a gull
and the cry of a gull?

I am a simple man come up
from the long stoop of the sea.
I have come a long way up the valley
to ask your prayers for me.

I come from shores where ships find rock
and stave all timbers in.
I come from cities loud as birds
where money runs like gin.

I've come the whole world round about
to climb up from the sea
and walk up to your cottage door
and ask your prayers for me.

I've come from the turning weaving tide,
come from the long long wave
to ask you for your prayers for me
and ask for all you have.

I ask for everything you have,
for prayer is everything,
and as I knock upon the door,
Oh, as I knock upon the door,
Oh as I knock upon your door,
you'll hear the last bird sing.

But what is the bird that sings so loud?
What is the bird that answers the knock?
when the sea is hushed
and the wind is hushed
and the summer a long ago thing?

Why do you come with your word from the sea
and a tale of waves and a talk of prayer?
Who are you who climb from the dark
with the gaze of a stone
and the smile of a stone?

Listen. How long have you listened?
Have you been listening long?
You know I have been talking to you
ever since your death began.

    ° °

A Ballad of Johnnie Question

For John McDonald

This for Johnnie Question
   who made man his mark,
travelled the live rails of his bone
   along the tunnelled dark.

This verse for his thin-boned wrist,
    for his two threadbare rooms,
the rented stair and the sour gaslight
    and the yellowstone.

And this verse for the Wanted Ads,
    the forms, the dotted lines,
the echoing Assistance Board,
    and for the wind and rain.

This for the wind and for the rain.
    He pocketed his pride,
knocked it against his only shilling
    at his manhood's side.

And for his manhood, this. He took
    his everywhere to heart,
rapped iron on the every wooden
    door that locked him out.

And the first answer said to him,
    "Responsibility.
You took your own life on your head,
    What must be, must be.

Accept and work." He turned aside.
    Upon the sooty stone
he saw the words, "God so loved man
    that man must love alone."

And the second answer was,
    "The wisdom of the State
demands mobility of labour,
    and a reasonable Rate.

Learn proportion." He turned back.
    Upon the civic wall
he saw the words, "God so loved man
    no man need love at all."

O who was Johnnie Question
    that was meek and shy,
walking the bare streets of his bones
    with a staring eye?

This verse for his half of bitter,
    for his leaking shoe,
the girl that bore his white children,
    and for the football queue.

And this verse for the pin-up
    and for the public name,
the statesman and the bulletin,
    and this for the wind and rain.

This for the wind and for the rain,
    and for his manhood this.
He knocked upon the door of all
    the old eternities.

The answer came. "To give to all
    that asked would ruin all."
He watched the ruined poster flap
    upon the churchyard wall.

The answer came. "The Charities
    and State may help you out."
O, who was Johnnie Question
    to make the faithful doubt?

O, who was Johnnie Question?
    What did he learn at school?
Upon the blackboard, "God is Love,
    Expediency, and Rule."

This verse for the answerers,
    and for the rich man's gate,
the Economist, the Politician,
    and for the Church and State.

And this for Johnnie Question,
    for his manhood shame,
the shilling knocking at his thigh,
    and this for the wind and rain.

        ⊙ ⊙

A Ballad of Despair

Mercy, Pity, Peace, and Love.
    I met a walking man.
He walked each street towards despair
    and stared up at the sun.

This way he walked. A sawdust head
    knocked on his coughing chest.
A hand twitched like an empty glove.
    A boot scratched at the dust.

"The Lamb that died," the preacher said.
    He saw the Lamb that died.
There was a black cloud round its head,
    a law book at its side.

"Love your neighbour," said the preacher,
    "and obey the Law."
He saw the blinded fishermen
    die on the green shore.

He saw his brother spitting sand
    with barbed wire round his head.
His hands like rags turned his door key.
    His mouth shone like lead.

He climbed the stair. At the first step
    he saw a city burn.
Children with flesh like trailing rags
    watched him from the turn.

The second step he took, the sea
    delivered up its dead.
The shoals of miles shone their white bellies
    at his staring head.

And the third step he climbed, he stopped.
    He stood stiff as a door.
A thousand blinded tongueless creatures
    coupled on the floor.

He stopped, then climbed. He went into
    the room his children lay.
He knew that he was mad as truth
    to take their lives away.

He knew that truth was mad. He walked
    the darkness of the street,
cried, "Suffer the little children
    to die in a clean sheet."

He climbed the headline steps outside
    the black industrial hall,
cried, "Though the children ask for bread,
    what bread is there not stone?"

What bread not stone? I met him dressed
    in pity and in blood.
I met him knelt in Calvary Place
    beside his children's bed.

Mercy, Pity, Peace, and Love,
    I saw him lift his gun.
He lay like logic in the street
    and stared at the blind sun.

        ❋ ❋

A Piece of Orange Peel

Coloured the incredible flame
of the blaze in a child's picture book,
skin pocked and pitted like the moon's,
it curls on the pavement, a pothook
of some giant scribbler whose word stopped
short of its comment and went slack.

The blinds are drawn. At the very end
fingers like sucked bones touched the Book
as touching wood; her shrill breath
reached for a word, but fell back;
her eyes gaped and then closed
on a blaze of pain that turned black.

The pith, scuffed, ragged, a torn swerve
of dirty yellow, spongy, sore,
has not yet dried; a film of dust
and specks of soot adhere where four
self-congratulating flies
settle and ticklishly explore.

All over, they closed her eyes
that had flicked open again to stare
on her first true blindness. Hands
washed, dried, dressed, combed the grey hair
that crackled and sputtered, the black Book
moved onto the bedside chair.

Kicked and downtrodden, the peel snaps;
blackened, crisped, and dried thin
as a lathe-shaving, it awaits
rainflood or broomstroke to begin,
and in another street the hands
that made it tear at skin again.

⚬ ⚬

The Street

Lost in the ordinary street, he turned
and stared up at the ordinary blinds,
and knocked, half-hearted, at a peeling door;
not that he thought he'd learn from the reply,
or even that he'd know to tell them why
he'd come this way, or what his walk was for.

No one replied or stirred. Nothing was changed.
No echo boomed. No shuffling slipper made
its apprehensive pause before the latch.
They'd gone away. He'd known before he knocked
the house was certain to be double locked,
and anyway all answers have a catch.

Lost in the ordinary pause before
the locked and peeling ordinary door,
he knew he'd meet no one the least surprised.
This was a common spectre of the street,
the broken shoes upon the aimless feet,
the absence, and the question, and the lies.

It wasn't that they didn't care to get
strangers or answers in the street, and yet
it wasn't accident the blinds were down.
Something had gone away. He could stay lost,
or telephone the police and ask the cost
of questioning every suspect in the town.

        ◦ ◦

Transport Café Crossword

Heavy and sad. A sad and heavy face
the colour of dirty sand. A rubbed-back cap.
Hair black as spanish. Stubble blue. Red hands.
He pushes back the plastic coffee cup
and broods upon the paper. Fourteen Down,
and N and M the only letters known.

Hunched as a man behind the wheel, his stub
of pencil jabbing down as he counts out
another false solution, he allows
his adversary to make every doubt
a matter for despair. *Moment* too short.
Momentary he ponders, and then scouts.

Looks at his watch unknowingly, and raps
the pencil for another cup. His gaze
about the room is abstract as a word
no-one has thought of yet, but through the haze
he nods at someone's grin. The cup's too hot.
It doesn't seem to care what game he plays

with N and M and Time. It makes him swear,
though absently. His massive head is leant
upon his hand. *No Usage Lasts Out Time*.
He thinks of years, of centuries, his bent
and brooding head carved out of stone, his hand
as still and lonely as a monument.

◦ ◦

House and Scholar

For Tony Connor

He thought of buying this old house,
in love with stone-flagged floors,
beams that retained the twist of the tree,
and a landscape melted by thick windows.

He pondered on the leisureliness of time
transforming time, conceiving monumental
order grown from ordinary lives,
their day-in-and-day-out renamed "traditional."

Something here had kept a kind of faith.
Taking a turn about the unkempt garden
(green pelt upon millpond, quince in orchard,
moss hillocked on the mounting block, earth sodden),

he felt that living here might be a way
of owning history, making no departure
from the long dead, answering their names
in their own language from an ignorant future.

Ghosts were half his mind. He had been talking
ghosts up now for what seemed like forever,
sipping his blood into their mouths. He picked
seeds from dead grass and told them like a lover.

But the house said nothing. Nothing spoke.
A nearing car replaced it in the past.
He watched a fringe of rain bead swollen eaves,
and all he could remember was the cost.

◦ ◦

John Arthur

John Arthur walks the tideline-scribbled sand,
having nothing else to do but let things slide,
driftwood, wreckage, weed kicked into mounds,
poked and prodded, taffled and let bide.

You'd think, his tar-smeared rain-stained mac
flapping at every slouched lunge of the knee,
he had a wisdom that we strangers lack,
some slow-tongued gnomon of sand, wind, and sea,

and was content. You'd think that if you could,
unwilling to believe him derelict,
walking beside great waters whose brown flood
roars down a wreckers' harvest to be picked –

kindling (of course) its staple, but much more
washed from the fat black coasters as they roll –
you'd figure him an uncrowned ignorant Lear
trapped on the blustered edges of the world,

and you'd be wrong all through, because John Arthur
has nothing else to do but let things slide;
driftwood and sunlight, weed and wanting, slither
endlessly through him like the sour brown tide,

and days are just for filling in with time.
Get closer and you'll see his sandblind stare.
One foot drags, one hand twitches, waves crash down
and mile and mile on mile destroy the shore.

    ◦ ◦

Joe Sampson

Waistcoat wrinkled brown as puddles,
chin scattered with bristling white,
cheeks red as good meat,
long gun under arm, he'd shot
the fox, caught it along the hedge
of North Field End and watched it drop.

In another county no reason
could have protected him – a bitch
heavy with young at that time of the year!
But Joe Sampson cleared thistle, vetch,
and fox with the same plough-logic; here
land must be conquered at all's cost.

Something there was in him honest, crude
as the turned clay's shined swerve
back of the plough, and something mocking
the cluttered sentiments round the grave
of any vermin, or used thing;
guns are beliefs a man must have,

each death a clearance of good land
and the land's decision. None were
boxed but rightly; none lived
except by land-rule. He closed the door
of the Bull, and leaned his shotgun up,
slapped the brush down on the bar.

⁕   ⁕

"Angel"

They called her "Angel," sardonic
at bitter scrubbing arm
sharp as a scraped white shinbone
there in the chicken run
for hens to clack at, mottled
brown by the rain and sun.

She was the sour-faced snatcher
at every gossip's tale,
bent graceless, thankless, angular,
over the clanging pail,
the wet wood rough with scrubbing,
the hot carbolic smell.

Yes, she was bitter, God knows –
bitter and sour and quick
to vex as a thistle blurting
its milk at a swung stick;
her head was a mortification
of curlers and twisted grips.

So "Angel" they called her, laughing.
Her son was a big lad,
simple and shy and clumsy.
If ever she had a glad
softness for him she kept it dark,
abused all the luck she had.

And died. But before that last
vengeful retort to breath
she saw him wed and settled.
"Poor Angel" they said at his wreath.
And the women removed the tight curlers
once she lay small in death.

＊　＊

Alison Jane Skelton

This infant staggerer carries round
in clutched fist doll and animal –
splayed ragged arms and flayed face,
chewed wet fur, torn paws. Her falls
are sudden squats on the claimed ground,
her lunges trials of guessed space.

Triumphant tyranny in her clutch
and huge cry shakes us to the heart;
the clenched assertion of her stare
and random language tugs apart
each easy sentiment; her pink
fat hands grub realistic floors.

Small pities have no place in her,
love a demand, intolerant, plain,
for food or service; tears dried,
withdrawn into her own again,
she tramples doll and animal
strewn carelessly across the wide

expanse of all the place she knows.
Can years bring alteration here,
or will she, in her private strength
of woman, keep this hidden near,
unknown of watcher, listener, friend,
or conquering lover, till, at length,

necessity and will combine
in summoning her to wake again
the pitiless tyrannic bent
of her own self-absorbment? Then,
will she be strong, who, small, is strong,
and force life to replenishment?

       ◦ ◦

Cat and Bird

"Kiss me, and if that is old hat
under the moon, be out of date
once in a while, because the tune
is one that has stayed up too late
and falls asleep upon its bars,
childish as kittens, and because
who was it said once every house
is roofed with platitudes like slate?
Kiss me," she said. I heard the cat
moving among the strawberries.

"Tell me, and if you can't think what,
having forgotten, take a shot
at someone's words because the day
here in this room is close and hot
and silence is as full of words

as all your books, and, oh, because
why was it that we bought this house
if not with an indecent thought?
Tell me," she said. I saw the bird
wounding the heavy strawberries.

"Always and always; that, if trite,
could still ring true if we had not
seen each way end, and now, because
we have grown tired of lying late
and early in this watchful house,
playful with memories, and because
we find all music runs to bars,
how long should we keep kisses caught?
Always?" she asked. The cat and bird
wrestled among the strawberries.

          ❂   ❂

Nothing of Beauty

Nothing of beauty
(watching the coarse flesh),
rather the relish
of a mutual, gross,
accepting knowledge:
what is true is use –
beauty, that nagging
midnight tooth, no loss.

Unless you gloss it
(clapping the two bones),
calling the need the beauty,
urging this
to leap philosophies
where many, thrown,
have broken backs
upon the stone that is.

Or if you make it
(gentling the used flesh),
rather the sharing
of the hungry ghost
no meat may gorge,
that stands aside, calls "Truth,"
"Love," "Beauty," "Peace,"
and is himself the lost.

       *   *

Sancreed Churchyard

Don't tell me that the grave's a fine
and private place if you would stand
beside me here. Each name is worn
never so boldly as upon the stone.
This miller with his round mill stone
snores till the clappers have outworn
all history. Then he will upstand,
though all the worms have eaten fine.

Don't kid me that the whistling bird
pules for some dear and huddled bones,
or that the rank flowers sweating in their glass
are fed with tears from a lamenting boy.
This docked and dandelioned boy,
hid in his green hump, has a glass
of yellow rainwater. His bones
think less of grief than feathers of a bird.

Put by your monotones. These words
were live enough and will come out
wearing their shames and trades to talk
your ordinary glories down.
That mossed cross may be fallen down,
that marble stained, but they will talk
how every weather kept tears out
though all the mourners drowned in words.

       *   *

An Uncertain Meaning

Wearing an old coat in the sweat of sun,
uprooting plantains from the not-so-level
length of lawn, the inevitable I
becomes sententious, moral, at the drop
of memory's thinking cap: uprooting all
(perhaps) of canker in the yeasty flesh,
grubbing up each guilt with blackened nails,
or else (another way to twist the key)
humbling the animal under furious light.

That's not what I set out to say. I thought
to send a message out of my sure love,
deliberate as heartbeats, a decorum
of the passionate order your name made,
but this broke in. Outside the sky is grey,
the sun invisible, the lawn still pinned
firmly down with plantains. I've not been
that gardener yet, not grubbed up anything
this ordinary February afternoon.

There may be no connection, or there may.
Ingenuity suggests the words
came from a hidden prompting, and my love
is less an order than an ordering
still setting innocence to rights, a beast
covered with all old dreams of hide and hair
working its heat out, struggling for a place
where penance has brought every kind perfection
and natural impulse lacks its natural flaws.

But such is to disguise the actual thing.
It is not certain what the symbols mean.
Likely enough it looked so cold outside
I had to wear death's coat below the sun
for emphasis of heat, and had to stoop
because the every thought is bedded deep,
and walked the lawn because the flesh is grass
and flesh is asking now. Or maybe not.
At any rate, I send this with my love.

⊙ ⊙

Begging the Dialect

For Christopher Hanson

The crumpled villages, guide-booked and mapped,
of a flat land by a flat sea, cold and wet,
mark my destination, caul in hand,
begging from door to door the dialect.

What is that? And that? And that? What did
your father call it? What his father? What?
The thin quick ribboning of the sentences
whirrs to record the pause, the slur, the act.

Broken and blurred, pitched out of the one key
to turn the wards round and unlock a place,
I play it back. You notice, if you look,
the old men all have the one watchful face

hardened like cart-ruts in a hard frost, made
all the same ridge and hollow. Playing back,
the lid reflects my darkly bended head
growing towards that sealed familiar mask

till I am asked, perhaps by my sons, What
do you call that? Call that? The spool runs out.
Back again, I haunt them, caul in hand,
begging from door to door the dialect.

⊙ ⊙

Riches

The ditch in Humber Lane
was black with tadpoles, round
black beads and whippy tails;
I knelt down at the side
and filled my jar as black
as now I fill this page,
glad of the gathered life,
however many died.

⊙ ⊙

Ancestors

Tame jackdaw on his head, my father
lived boyhoods of stolen apples,
pawky curates, and drunk farmers;
slingshot in stackyards fed his owls
caged in the loft. Jack, black
as the ace of spades, mocked all comers;

made away once with a man's watch
(none of your trinkets, a gold hunter
well cased and fobbed), was at last lost
and no heart to catch another.
Tales of the Wolds. My father's tales,
his father being the schoolmaster.

Those were titanic years still
in the Nineties. My Grandad's first bike
was the first for the Wolds. Some bad spills.
At an advanced age he learned Greek
to tease the parson, at service time
followed the lesson by the Book.

It was he, too, sending the boys off
to gather strawberries, said, "Whistle!
If you once stop, I'll be along! "
No aphorism of the apostle
or phrase of a great man ever stuck
so firm as that legendary tattle.

And his father? The tale stops.
I only know he had many sons
and some daughters that took his wealth,
and there are some shaky tales that run
on how he brought rail to the east coast,
but, I think, garbled. Of details none.

So the story ends in a figure big
with the upland mist, who could trace back
himself, no doubt, to a great house.
There was money once, it is said. But Jack
is the clearest image. He thieved time
as my father apples, way back

there in the place where whistling proved
a trick of the innocence they loved.

The Brig

It was six foot four of my father
balanced upon the jag
of the green-brown rock with his bright rod
after the long drag
round from the bay over weed-raked pools
that made me see the Brig.

His hair was white as the flying spume,
his hand as hard as wood,
his eyes blue as the blue pool
that mirrored how he stood,
holding within its depthless rock
sky-space, man, and flood.

Inverted there like a totem hung
down into the sky
where spectral gulls involved the weed
with gaping soundless cry,
he fished a far unbeing sea
no man might profit by.

I watched him, back towards the pool,
cast out into the foam
beyond the ledge of rock on rock;
I watched him stand alone,
one man as tall as any tower,
and one deep as stone.

⊚   ⊛

Land without Customs

For John Montague

My land had no customs. Habits, tricks
of the slow tongue, leading beasts to grass,
road slape with rain, or answering
weddings and deaths in a dry voice
scurfy as dust in the village square,
boys' names carved in the old stocks;

these – but no customs. Unless you count
the old men making one stretch of wall
the place for their backs, spring sun
blinking their eyes; or the way all
was marbles one day, the next tops,
in the road alongside the brick school.

Certain inevitables there were: the rub
of hands on apron at house door
to speak to strangers, the mild horse
surging the plough at a harsh roar
of ritual violence, the long silence
before speech. And these were

known and unknown. The land stood
somewhere inside them. A phrase missed,
a nod too easy, and boots dragged
at embarrassed cobbles. Two miles west
it was shallower, lighter. I once saw
a man there run for the town bus.

But no customs. In a way stronger
for that, I think. There was no need
to assert the place. It grew, changed;
the electric came and a new road
out to the south, and the telephone.
The pump was condemned. But the past stood.

And I daresay still, in its own way,
stands. Though a plaque by the old stocks
set in the wall is a thought strange,
there in the square are the old looks,
the pause before speech, the drab men
spitting in dust. Should I go back,

these will have made me. The small fields
are as small elsewhere, the sky as blue
or just as grey with a thread of rain,
the stacks as lumpish, but here grew
something inalienable, a way
of giving each least thing its due,

a rock to living. A land without
customs, yes, but a land held

hard on its course, unsparing, firm
in its own ways. As I grow old
time hardens into that sure face
watching the foreign, shiftless world.

⊚   ⊚

Message for my Father

I'm never certain what the message is
except that it is quiet and in words.
I watch you bending by the apple tree,
the white cloud massive as a watching head,
the dark earth gentle. Maybe time compels.
Or maybe time is all we have to spare.

I used to climb, once, a particular tree
under a stack side, and its upper twigs
wore straws clawed from the stack. And there I'd slide
and slither down most days, adept at falls
on to the gold ground, breathless, jumping up
to climb again and slide down from the sky.
But the tree. I think that it was bare,
or nearly bare, the mossed bark knuckled through,
the twigs dry. Certainly there were no apples.
Yet it lived. Transfigurations talked
crowded as sparrows in its bitten leaves.
If it had leaves. I can't remember quite.
Yes, leaves there must have been, for there was shade
poppling my face in sunlight. I would pick
one leaf and keep it like a word from home.

And so it comes round to it, slowly round,
nearing the message – if the leaf will speak,
if words and memories can be retrieved.
You're standing now, and easing your stiff back,
watching the Worcester Pearmains change the sky.
Yet how am I to say . . . what can't be said
except by silence? I talk silence out
until it comes back filled with every phrase
of hesitation, every false start,
the passion, the inquiry, and the love.

⊚   ⊚

As I Remember It

As I remember it, the place was old;
a fingernail pressed home into the wood
black-wet with autumn could scoop yellow cheese
that squashed like pith of elder in the hand;
wood-shavings, pitch-pine mostly, lay around,
the top layer fresh and crispy, faintly rose,
the ones below brown, sodden. Saw and axe
lay on a fruit box with a sharpening stone,
and everything was still. As I remember,
trees drooped stiff outside, and there was rain.

The Shed, they called it. "Gone down to The Shed"
answered most callers of an afternoon.
Beyond the kitchen garden where the mud
from heavy boots had tramped the grasses down
to make a track, it sagged beneath the wind,
lopsided, flapping felt along one edge
of the half-hearted roof. The window – square
as nothing else was square – had on its ledge
a jam jar and five rusty nails a nudge
would always lose upon the stamped clay floor
among the shavings. On a hook a sickle,
rusted beyond belief, rocked at the door's
imperfect closing. Now I think of it,
there was a postcard pinned upon the door.

As I recall, it was from foreign parts –
I think a square with pigeons and a sky
more blue than possible, all shine and gloss,
and ill-shaped people promenading by;
the front was scratched, one corner tattered; why
the thing was pinned there heaven only knows.
As I remember it, I pulled it down.
It's odd how a chance memory grows and grows.

The card was at the back of it. The card
it was that set me thinking of The Shed,
and yet I almost missed it – small and bright,
its drawing pins rusted home into the wood.

The other side told nothing. All it said
was "With Best Wishes" and the name was blurred
beyond all understanding, while the stamp
had gone long since. The whole thing was absurd.
And yet, as I picked up the nails again,
I felt a private glory had occurred.

⚬ ⚬

Poem on His Thirty-Fifth Birthday

Halfway to where God only knows,
is it a trick like the ant's scuttle,
this all-for-Art, this home-making,
to end on the dump, a used bottle?

All's made in belief that what stays
somewhere around when boxed down
is more than a smell of old cheese,
a torn postcard flushed in the drain,

but is it more? Bones of my father
in me maybe, but his own creaking,
stiffening, soon rid of. A good Dad
in terms of a good there's no checking.

Immortal I heard first at round five
meant harps and wings and Nobodaddy,
drew God on some paper and crossed him out
like writing rude words in the privy.

And later Immortal was words. Then
was it I started up? Eleven,
I made my first poem about the sea,
recall I felt curiously forgiven.

Searching that out brings more up.
I never really believed in the dead
till Aunt Agnes was small wax
in the front parlour, voice ended.

Or was it the guinea-pig, the snake
with its head crushed, crimson and green,
or the kittens that left the bucket clay,
cold wet gloves with the bones still in?

Backwards is forwards in this. To look
at the learnt deaths no more than a guess
at whose ending? Not mine! Not mine!
The essential I escapes the mess.

And escapes it where? Back to thirty-five,
half-way to never, the old wheel
rutting its journey till spokes shiver
into an absolute of the real?

Or cloud-pink, hymn-sick goody-where,
everyone loving, and God big
as a child's Christmas, outside
atheists getting over their jag?

Or maybe the bigger subtler words –
Life-Force, World-Soul, one with One:
burying one's head in this paper bag
is no way to get history done.

And something, God alone knows what,
must get done somehow. Why so?
God knows that too, if He exists,
or can know at all, being out of the show.

So we get nowhere. That's where we get.
A lemming's gallop, an ant's scuttle,
preserving the race of lemmings, ants.
Our children demand we lose the battle.

Now, however, I make truce;
today take stock, pause, reload.
I can't win, but I'll see I set
time a tough proposition, by God!

First, I have taught a few hundred
to teach some thousands the wrong things,
disrupting the state with good verse,
bad scholarship, and hard drinking.

Second, I've brought a few poets up
to distrust literature, and keep
obscenity handy for bad laws,
prigs, and academic sheep.

Third, I've defeated a sly hope
of foozling my way to Reputation
by telling the truth at least some of the time,
and always on unsuitable occasions.

Fourth, I have made poems – good, bad,
indifferent, mystical, obscene –
that someone may want when I am dead
to keep off the guilt and the bad dream.

Four. And that's all. I make no claim
for helping the tribe with fine kids.
Good or bad, I'm too much stuck
on the way they are young to make bids.

I can't say I've ever done a good deed
out of the common. I've passed by
beggars and charities and pain
with a full pocket and a dry eye.

I've kept no commandment I can recall,
having killed by proxy and by word
and broken the rest in good style,
scorning my neighbour, and cursing God.

Not much of a record. And what's ahead?
Poems till I drop, and words, words,
words. It's my trade. The black keys
clicking the tragic and the absurd.

And maybe some change. When the blood thins
I will die a little, and grow old
as gracelessly as I can to keep
some heat against the ultimate cold.

No more than that. I ask no praise,
and beg no comfort, my one prayer
I keep my heart and wit enough
to get me God alone knows where.

◦　◦

Two Moralities and a Footnote

I

In a shop advertised as selling "Aids
to Better Vision" (scorning the low term "glasses"),
the portrait, horn-rimmed, of a poet looks down
on all the myopoeia that passes,
thinking of something else, no doubt, but not
(I dare assume) the symbolism of sight –
more probably how that one's hair is gold
and this one's skirt deliriously tight.

II

Last night we played the animal. Today
I hear you singing to the children. "There,"
I think, "she goes! " It seems I muscled in
on private tunes which, glad to have me share,
you now make free confession of; our feet
were mingled to that sweet barbaric air.

And yet tonight I'll greet, man being brute,
eyes not quite virginal, though make-up chic,
smart shoes, smart handbag, and conspiring grin
boasting the curly fleece this Jason seeks
with hardening muscle, and, as we begin,
will hear the same tune hissing through her teeth.

III

You condemn this Muse, but yet, observe,
it was Her finger on the climbing nerve
that played the tune old blinded Homer wrote
of History with its mouth on Helen's throat.

   *   *

Quaternion for the Muse

I

Seeing her in her various disguises,
broad wife, black-sheathed schoolgirl, swinging tart,
blonde, brown, lissom, squabby, moist-eyed, dozy,
how can he tell realities apart
enough to know which one will fit his crown
and drag across the stage Her blinding curtain?
Only the unsought, unthought, strange-eyed bitch
will plague that itch and make his verses certain.

II

Offend her, if you must, with random women,
drink, drugs, thievery, or lay nations waste –
these she may tolerate as venial, but
once boast of cunning or inflate your taste
into a principle of separate rule,
you'll feel the downturn of that sovereign hand,
and, old or young, cold scholar or hot fool,
will tumble, gaunt and wordy, with the damned.

III

This man who is dead made poems.
                              Now on his grave
I scatter public leaves, gloss-darkened holly,
spotted laurel, blue-green ferns of yew,
woven into a hubless, spokeless, holy
wheel — the usual dismissive token
of the turning year, and of completion.

But the Angel sorrowing above stone
in stone humility his heirs provide
I give no leaf to; she leans, gravely dressed
in robes and misery, who should bestride
this huddle, arms akimbo, out-thrust hips,
bared breasts, wild hair, triumphant parted lips.

IV

Wrestle this Angel, and whoever falls
to head-lock, arm-lock, hip-tilt, threshing thigh,
it is Her victory, or none at all.

Hers is that last, wild, conquering, plundered cry.

     ✹ ✹

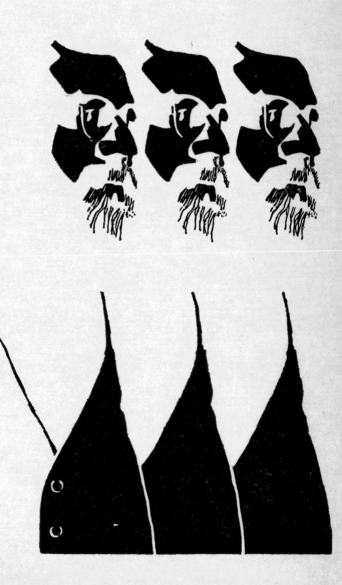

A First Ballad of the Muse

You, the listener, listen.
I stand where words begin
and time is called. Come over to
the snug I'm harboured in.
My nails of heels tack down the black
and glisten of the street,
and I'm the one original whore
that sweats the winding sheet.

I call you quietly and slow.
Time is a strange strange thing.
You spin a history out and find
the history begin.
You flip a penny memory and
go in at your own door,
and there a new conclusion lies
and stares up from the floor.

Come over here and name your want.
The blowfly crawls the wall.
Names are the only lonely watchers
when your apples fall,
and we'll be one name in the dark,
as in the dark love lies
flat up against the window catch
that rattles at the skies.

We'll spell one word this cocksure night.
You'll have your sentence fling
its small-shot at my belly's shout
the drill hall we'll be in;
I'll have you sentry quick as wink
and grip your gun like rock;
I wear my breasts as armament
and fight each night I look.

I put your word into my mouth
and spell your sentence bare.
A bright bone button winks at you
up from the bedroom floor.
The creased cloth grins. The hot sheet shifts.

We meet in one wide bed.
The blowfly crawls the knocking wall
and the great word is said.

It's shouted out. Come closer, dear;
I know my voice is raw
as any waiting twice-timed bitch
that has you in her door,
but o that husky edge you hear
is what the women cry
who ply short-time in the arcade
and know the hearse go by.

For time is short. I talk about
what every man jack's found,
locked in the threadbare winding sheet
with woman and with wound.
But I'm not hiring minutes out.
You have the need I am.
We meet in one where the knife hangs up
above the tangled ram.

We meet in one. One is our name.
The blowfly crawls the wall.
But names knit where that Madame smiles
her knife blade on us all;
though I'll drive deep your bargain
and not a penny's found,
we beat upon the black full point
that blocks us in the end.

Bed down with me and you'll not get
your lonely name again.
My tongue will talk your muscle down
and my throat speak your pain.
My hand will cramp your sentence out,
my thighs dream in your bed,
and my black nails of heels tack down
the pavestones of your dead.

Give me your look. That eye you have
will find the deep of me,
but look me back into the eye
and I'll own all you see.
You'll walk my pitch and clack my heels

and fumble buttons back
from all the generations that
would have you on your rack.

Step over here. I am your Fate –
you're fated to a whore.
And there's no scented night-dress hanging
up behind my door,
no midnight pool or pink champagne,
but what's beneath my skirt
is common knowledge, and I am
as common as the dirt.

Common is the word I am,
and I am that to all.
Step over here and take your chance
to have your apples fall.
Stake your luck deep and it will turn
within the tossing bed;
the blowfly walks the knocking wall
till the last word is said.

The blowfly crawls the brothel wall.
The clock winks like a pin.
The shortest time is long enough
to get your one word in.
The shortest time is double-backed
to let the sentence spend
until we come upon the black
that blocks us in the end.

The black full point. I am. You are.
A syntax shakes the house.
Words are what lean us up against
the separating glass.
My nails of heels tap gravestones down
until the gravestones call.
I am the word man had at first
and shall have when I fall.

⊚   ⊚   ⊚

Ballad of a Mine

*The Wheal Owles mining disaster occurred in
the early years of this century when the miners
broke through into an adjacent flooded mine
called Come Lucky. Nineteen men and a boy
were drowned, and the sole survivor from the
working where the accident took place walked
the roads of West Penwith as a pedlar for the
remainder of his life. The shoring up of the
workings with pit props is known in Cornwall
as "keeping the country abroad." At a museum
in Zennor, there is a miner's lamp inscribed with
the words "Goodbye the day. Good luck to me."*

Between Botallack and the light
I took the lamp below,
the tunnelled summers of the mind
black and sour as sloe.
The daybreak brought the darkness down;
at day's end night was free
to dowse the lamp that carried down
"Goodbye the day. Good luck to me."

You have to go a long way round
to have a history told.
For twenty years I've seen the lifted
white head of the road
that hills it up Nancherrow side
frown grey as a carn
and held my tongue against its spate
to keep disaster warm.

Nineteen steps up to the gate,
and half a nineteen more.
I count the steps in those men's names
who faced the waters' roar.
Nineteen years and a bit.
(The bittock was a lad.)
It goes a long way round about
to get a learned thing said.

Wheal Owles above the burning sea
that dazzles out the eye
of any man who knows the night
mine down into the day,
we bent to break the clagged ore out
while breath was harsh as scree
and sweat sloped down the buttock back.
Goodbye the day. Good luck to me.

I've never had a dream of what
the first great morning said
when the bag of water broke
for man to breach his head,
or when my father first set down
my name within his mind,
and swung his lamp down at the door
warped with the wet sea wind.

I've never had a word come in
the hollow of the dark
to tell the first great watcher's word
who broke life from the rock,
though then it was a thing enough
and all the folk stood round
as they stood at Wheal Owles the day
I got the chapter learned.

Learned me the chapter, that day did.
Nineteen paces more.
Nineteen and a bittock
from this door to that door.
What I have here I have to sell.
With breath as harsh as scree
we bent to break the black ore out.
Goodbye the day. Good luck to me.

We kept the country well abroad.
The road was clear as gin.
There was no crack or rotten tack
the working we were in.
Come Lucky nudged us on one side
but that was flooded out,
a house of water, and a house
we asked no visit at.

Come Lucky. But we have our luck.
Nineteen and a bit
your garden hedges by the road;
I've learned the length of it
from tread and tread for half a life,
the half of life let free
from mornings carrying down the shift
"Goodbye the day. Good luck to me."

Goodbye the day. Come Lucky lay
and nudged us in the pit.
A dead man took the steel drill up
and had his luck of it.
A pinhole. But a prick, a pin.
The crack starred out like light.
Light water-black. The wall of black
clapped like a Canaanite.

I think it was the prophet gave
that man's discovery back.
It was a nation served by flood
that saw the splitting rock.
But we have served no waters' way
but moled below God's sea.
And on the mole the mountain fell.
Goodbye the day. Good luck to me.

Ran like a river down the latch
and sneck of deadman's door,
broke like a bag of thunderclap
upon the carn-cragged moor,
alive and kicking, wombed with flood,
nineteen and a lad
spun round, spun round, the long way round
to say their history dead.

The country was well kept abroad.
I ran through waters' house.
The great wave, shouldered like a moor,
tore all heaven loose,
and at the crack of night came luck.
The black wet let me be.
The ladder held into the shaft.
Goodbye the day. Good luck to me.

The ladder held into the shaft
and this head met the sky.
Nineteen years and a bit
I've walked the history dry.
Nineteen men and but a lad.
Did darkness break that one might see?
I learned the chapter off by heart.
Goodbye the day. Good luck to me.

      ❂   ❂   ❂

Ballad of the Four Fishers

For Michael and Margaret Snow

I got four sons across my bed
below the harbour wall,
and April slid like silver eels
when I was marrying tall;
though bells and bells and bells rocked out
above the piled-up town
four sons jumped in my star-splayed loin
and all my wounds were drowned.

"Turn to time's other side," he said;
"You'll have your net-mesh swag
with heavier leaping fish than any
unblessed nets could drag;
you'll haul it full." Nine months I hauled;
the bag of waters broke:
whose was the voice I recognized
when my own belly spoke?

I got four sons. They gave me all
that flesh and blood could bear.
The holy dust ran like a mouse
below the churching door.
Sands scuttled fast as winds blew up
before He blessed each head;
the name-words tasted in my mouth
of the red salt of blood.

If you've seen stars out on a night
the rocked boats' moorings twitch,
gulls idling white upon the black,
or, troubled by time's itch,
walked corkscrew streets on to the top
to stare down on the town
and watched the one by one lamps snuff
the one by one blinds down;

if you've walked back from tides to find
the wet slap of the fish
flipping its flat white belly on
the friday of the dish,
the lifted hands clasped cockle-stiff,
the given thanks, you've known
the lifted hook of every wave
can gaff you to the bone.

Nets on the rails, and walls of webs,
nets written on the wind;
I took the black book of the rock
as anchor for my mind.
I took the bent moon for my ring,
the big sail for my sheet,
but death strung nets out like a drift
across the climbing street.

The islands knocked their holes in tides;
the great cliffs locked their door.
I heard the clapper-trap of gulls
shout on the shell-bright shore.
But winter stiffened skies to wood
and nailed them on the eye.
I had four sons come home from sea
and only one was dry.

The fishbox houses crowd me round,
the windows black as rocks.
The gulls scream round the harbour sky;
the ropes scream through the blocks.
I wake up from the sleep of breath
and breath chokes breath like mist
within the crying of the gulls
that my three sons have kissed.

I walk in Virgin Street alone
through nets like cataract;
the watchers on the drystone steps
are dressed in fisher black.
I walk out by the iron pier
that straddles the used sand,
and tidals of the thigh and breast
turn on the lover's hand.

Roust out your prayers and mercies now
to tailor weeds for grief;
I split the word jammed in my jaws
with time's scaled gutting knife.
I lay my child-torn belly on
the friday of the stone;
the elder clasps his cockle hands
and all my grace is done.

Nets write their frenzied scribbles out
upon the gull-shrill air;
my one son looks out on the sea
and knows his muscles stir.
He turns his wrist upon the wood
as time turns in my side.
The shoaling cards fall like a wave
and spill his fortune wide.

Put back the cards; they slide like fish
and spell the same deep end.
I'd walk the eel-sleek shine of waters
to His blessing hand,
but shuttles tear the netting fingers
till the cord is cut.
I touched the black book of the rock
and found my heart was wet.

My heart a sea, deep, green and black,
my fingers whitened shell,
my eyes blind as the blinded thing
that pulses the dumb pool,
and my wits cut, his oars rove through
the trammels of the sea.
I had four sons got by the tide
and tides have broken three.

I had four sons across my bed
below the weed-green wall;
under the hunting of the gulls
you'll hear their voices call,
and one and one and one again
they sweep across my eye:
blind hands reach to the blinding sea
and my grey belly dry.

      ◉   ◉   ◉

Ballad of Billy Barker

A gay young widow woman
with eyes as green as glass,
and a bandy-legged prospector
with slum upon his ass;
you split your sides to think of it,
but I lie stiff as stone:
it's curtains now for English Bill
in Victoria Old Men's Home.

On Williams Creek in August
back in sixty two
the claims ran dry. The black sand let
no speck of colour through.
Ned Stout came down the canyon
and found his gulch and struck;
I followed him, staked out my claim,
and drove down through the rock.

Jumped ship, I did, and followed up
the blinding yellow dream.
The Fraser lashed its rolling stones
till mud was silver cream;
the walls of Hell's Gate cliffed me in
and Jackass Mountain shook
its dirt-brown back in mockery as
I trailed to stake my luck.

Seven of us worked that shaft.
The sun danced with the heat.
Ten feet we went and nothing showed.
Ten feet and then ten feet.
At thirty feet the cloud came up;
the sky was solid lead;
the windlass juddered at each hoist;
the wind sobbed for the dead.

Seven of us choked for breath.
I went down in the pit.
At forty feet the rain came down;
we took another foot.
A crazy sailor and six men
hauled rope till they were blind;
at fifty feet no colours showed
and even hope was mined.

Hope, Faith, Prayer were all mined out
and rubble piled up high
around the shaft-house hacked out from
the pines that hacked the sky;
mud welled; rain swaled; ropes cut and slid,
and heart and mouth were dry.

At sea the waters curve away
green satin from the bow,
and foam as thick as milk swirls out
along the track we plough,
and waves heave tall as hills and fall
like hills upon the deck.
The hills that stood round Williams Creek
would neither bend nor break.

The hills that frowned their forest black
above our hunch and sweat
rocked no horizons for our eyes,
nor shone out in the night
with greens and blues and grains of gold
as I've seen on the sea.
We took another foot. The dream
stood shuddering over me.

The yellow dream, the blinding dream
I'd taken for my life
stood over me. I felt its breath.
Its eyes cut like a knife.
I took another foot. Time stopped.
I heard it end my life.

I heard it finish, and I struck.
Five dollars to the pan;
and seven men on Williams Creek
went crazy to a man.
A thousand dollars every foot
we took out from that clay
and seven men on Williams Creek
were blinded by the day.

Drinks we had. Three days we drank
and all on English Bill.
I think I drank a thousand lives
at every swig and spill,
a thousand miners trailing north,
a thousand narrow pits
upon the benches by the creeks
where golden bones would sit.

I think in every glass I saw
a face and then a face;
a woman with long yellow hair
leaned into my embrace,
a widow with eyes green as grass
and lips as red as blood,
but at her back another face
as black as the wet wood.

Another face as black as wood,
with skin as soft as slum
and eyes as blind as pebbled quartz,
and gaping mouth as dumb
as Blessing's mouth, or Barry's mouth
that opened as he swung.

I met her in Victoria by
the bitter chilling strait;
some traded skins; I traded gold
and traded for a mate,
a London widow woman
and her golden hair and luck:
I took her up the Fraser
through the roaring mocking rock.

I took her up to Barkerville;
I should have let her be.
The gold ran out; the claim ran dry;
she ran loose as the sea;
her greens of satin, foams of silk
heaved up to prow on prow:
the sea's a wicked smother, but
I know a worse one now.

The sea's a wicked country;
its green hills lift and drown:
but earth's a played-out working
when you've thrown your money down.
I worked as cook; I begged; I washed;
my pans were grey with stone:
it's curtains now for English Bill
in Victoria Old Men's Home.

It's headstones now for English Bill.
My drinking roaring mouth
burns cancer where her kisses burned
and has a graver drouth,
and as I gape I see her face,
but then that other face
that looked on me in Williams Creek
and rotted like the race—

the race of men that dragged their packs
up canyons to the creek,
the race that heard my pick crack down
into that yellow strike,
whose deaths built law and church and state
upon my broken stone,
but Billy Barker's dead and gone
in Victoria Old Men's Home.

● ● ●

A Second Ballad of the Muse

Slip me the question of your need.
She walks the wakeful street
dressed up to undress your shaking
metric in her sheet.
O tart and sweet her high heels clack
the paved and asking stones
to shake her window-shopping ass
at every lust you own.

Oh yes, I know my words are coarse
as any groper's hand
locked in the doubling darkness with
a woman to be manned,
but what's the use of prettying up
the black cap of the law?
She walks the sensual street to die
the bought deaths of the whore.

O whore she is and tricked to kill.
The rustling shower coat
shines wetly as she swings her hips
along the stilt-heeled street.
Tricked out to kill, she'll die tonight
and any hour you pray.
O give your ghost a rendezvous
and muscle it away.

She is the fancy tart that knows
the fetish and the whip,
can fall each wrestler appetite
that burns you in its grip;
Goddess, child, queen, beast, and clown,
she has a greenroom thumb
to play out every act of breath,
but her last act is dumb.

Over behind the mammoth store
or by the boneyard wall
you'll find her leaning up against
the quiet of us all.

O call her on the telephone
and have a blinded date,
or meet her by the rain-black statue
and lose all you get.

Stand at the corner of time's street
and chance her sentence come.
As casual as an offered match
the huge disasters drum.
Imagination breaks your heart
while truth's paraded lies
high-heel their sweet sixteenings past
with down-lashed sidelong eyes.

O send her a letter scrawled with X.
Book the hotel room.
Time is the one she'll cheat you with
when you leave her alone.
Time is the stranger padding up
the rented winding stair
to find her listening for the key
with her white body bare.

O Time's the stranger smiling as
you squire her paid-up charms;
and Time's is that black scented glove
she lays upon your arm;
and Time's the fancy gentleman
that taught her how to please
and let your casual fingering linger
on her expensive knees.

Nylons rasp the furtive palm.
The shining belt unlocks.
There's meaning in the meantime mouth
that tongues her speaking looks.
The phrasing silks slip down her thighs.
The breasts of words elide.
This is the telling moment and
the told word breaks the bride.

Tickle her fancy if you can
or catch her on her day
and for the anything you give

she'll give herself away,
and easy is as easy does,
but, O, the cost is dear
when she stands in the coffin door
and asks the wage of fear.

Stood in the coffin doorway with
her high heels and her bag,
she lifts her black gloves to her lips
and takes a heavy drag;
she blows the smoke out on the night
that sailors tell her by,
and prophecies like black spent matches
ruin the wide sky.

O I've paid up and I've paid down
and found the bargain dear.
The body bared will burn you if
your lust wakes out of fear.
The naked flesh will scald your side,
the tongue destroy your tongue,
if you take thought of any cost
as her word is begun.

Expensive and expendable
as any appetite,
the bell-push nipples jut out hard,
the naked arms hold tight;
the syllabling of thighs cries out
till the great verb appals.
O body is how body dies
to answer that last call.

O body is when body dies
to have that word descend.
Strip in the syntax of her smile
and she'll spell out your end;
she'll burn your vision through her verb
until all meanings crack,
but Time is the lodger on the stair
and her last word is black.

    • • •

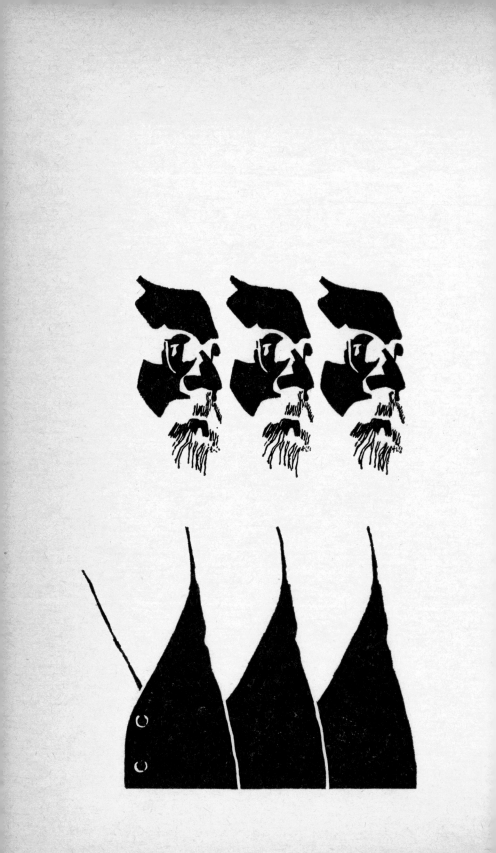

Undergrowth

I journey backwards.
Ahead is nothingness.
At forty-one
there's little in the mind
but thoughts of origins,
a primal speck,
the clutching branches
of a falling tree.

I hack my way through undergrowth.
Some girls
prefer an older man:
their loves are tight,
their nipples urgent;
out on Clover Point
the split moon spills
its monies in the sea

and through my slippery fingers.
I can't hold
the minute any more;
each windscreen swipe
rubs out the possible:
I see her home,
become her father
gnashing in his grave.

What was is where you are.
Who could take on
that cluttered fury?
Dreams and limitations
choke the tangling light.
I see my first
girl staring from
a stiff-necked photograph

with pigeons at her back.
Upon his column
rigid Nelson
wets his one blind eye
nostalgically.

Yellow dusk descends.
I choke upon a
twenty-year-old fog

and stagger farther.
Here one is alone.
The ruined summer-house
remembers crimes
against the spiders;
wasps blaze in a jar
hung from the warped
suggestion of a twig,

and summer is all springtime.
Flickering here,
the images move fast;
the little deaths
reduplicate and blur;
the books become
a single story
playing out the gods'

heroic roles and masteries,
conquering nettles
taller than my thigh.
I stumble, drop
upon the warm crisp grass;
within me, echoes
mesh and alter;
everything's at odds

still in this garden world,
though, dreaming forwards,
energy becomes itself
and time
a countless multitude.
Crowds hurry past
on backward journeys,
faces dark, confused,

ridiculous. The tree's
about to fall.
The undergrowth is filled
with scurrying cries.

◎   ◎   ◎   ◎

Lines for a Lady

E chi vedesse com' ella n' e gita,
Diria per certo: questa non ha vita.
(CAVALCANTI)

Remove your sleeping mask.
The drug is over.
Curtains heave to the slow push of the wind,
troubling their weighty flowers,
shifting rings
upon the long brown gleaming of the pole,
as dresden wriggles pastoral unquiet
on the death-cold marble beneath the mirror.

Shower now
in the ill-shaped converted bathroom
with the de Morgan tiles and the plastic curtain.
Adopt the face of the day
and gently sever
each retaining filament of evasion,
thus to accept the telegraph of the headlines,
the advertisements of destruction,
as a small
disquietude of elsewhere.
Death is listening
at the dead end of the telephone

you had disconnected for the night,
fearing the thin high voices,
the narrowing questions.
Re-connect now:
speech is frail by daylight;
fed by darkness, it is a different matter,
even a kind of nightmare,
the bodiless voices
tugging the pulse like elastic,
the one wrong voice
dragging the mouth down
at each sag of the curtain,
reminding cold of fingers smoothing the marble.

Now there is talk
like a cramped limb stretching the muscle,
easing and turning.

Dial, therefore, by memory.
It will ring.
The voice that answers will be harmless, light
in its understating renewals, its courteous rightness.
The heavy curtains are open on sliding rings,
and daylight stains your wrap;
there's nothing finished
by perfection, nothing the day won't stain
or the night escape.
                          Make your appointment.
There is a message pad by the telephone.

⊙　⊙　⊙　⊙

The Come-Back

I walk my reappearance
round these streets
with a familiar terror.
What remains
could be more than it was.
A greasy pavement
slithers my nervous feet
in expected rain.
Mount Preston. The
Particular Baptist Chapel.
The flat was, surely,
a little further on.

It smelt of cat and gas;
my unmade sheets
stayed on the bed for weeks;
I never made
real contact with the laundry;
my clothes were damp
and baths impossible:

you'd think that I'd
still recognize it, but
they look the same.
One of the three is
boarded up and dead.

That could be it. But
then, perhaps not. I can't
re-live what might be
somewhere else. I'm locked
out properly here;
impossible to claim
nostalgia for a house that
will not look
familiar, for all the
times it gripped
me in dark hallways.
Quickly, I turn my back,

uneasiness nearing dread.
"It isn't fair"
sounds like a child's whine
in my head. I trace
out doubt a route towards
the echoing rock-
encrusted house at the corner
of Cromer Terrace;
my basement room's still there;
I stoop and peer.
New furniture. New books
piled on new floors.

The floor had to be new.
It broke beneath me
thirteen years ago.
A mist of dry
brown spores masked every
polished surface, choking
throat and lung until
one comic day
the whole thing just caved in.
"Dry Rot," they said.
Little is left for Memory
to hang on by,

and I don't ask or knock.
Why knock, why ask?
This different place contains
a different ghost
that stoops and scribbles
as if he were meant
more than the rest of us,
and more possessed,
inquiet, certain. He
lifts up his head.
I walk away through rain
to lose a past

I dare not say Goodbye to.
This last house
I lived in is, I see,
waste ground, stamped flat.
It hardly troubles me
more than to clutch
my raincoat closer.
Somewhere else has thought
Odysseus dead, that's all.
One Spring I moved
house, muse, life, love,
along here in a handcart.

     ◎ ◎ ◎ ◎

City Varieties, Leeds, 1963

The last time I drank here
I saw Tod Slaughter
play *The Demon Barber*.
He'd run back
between deaths to the Circle
Bar for gin.
Jenny was seventy then.
Was it five hundred
times, or over a thousand
he'd done her in?

His great long face
was flabby-white, his voice
a different resonant
century's, his head
magnificent. I've always
played it straight.
You have to play these
grand things straight, he said.

We played ours almost straight,
but the run was shorter.
Once a year for three years
we played *Drink,*
A Dripping Saga through
the streets. I wore
a black top hat, moustache,
and cloak. They cheered,
hissed, laughed, and threw
tomatoes. We drank beer

and chased the girls.
Does that big blonde remember
my hand on her plump
bare tits beneath her mac,
walking back up Tonbridge
Street? And was it
that year the rotten fruit
finished off my cloak?

Dust dries my throat.
I have another Bass
on long dead lusts and
gaieties. No need
to burlesque their absurdities;
play them straight,
walking back from the bar
into the glow
of your nostalgia, enter,
gesture, wait,

and sound the heroic
statement. Love and Death
attend the slithering wigs
and wooden swords.

The Barber smiles. Time stops.
His razor lifts.
And from the Gods we
thunder daft applause.

    ◦ ◦ ◦ ◦

The Word

This worn-out word,
a battered bag
lumpy with protestations,
unguents, dreams,
shudders its slow bulk
interposed between
the frantic message
and the reaching arms.

What can one do with it?
How circumvent
the smell of hide,
the weight of lexicons?
Kicks break the foot or bury it.
Contemplation
heaves its maw apart
and spills out things

beyond prediction –
corners of dark rooms,
a rose bush by a gate,
a smear of lace
stuck to the monstrous skin,
a swollen breast,
larksong shrilling
above depths of grass.

It is unconquerable
and futile, muddling
crazed sobrieties
with rational games;
it is the treacherous
obstacle in which
we name the race, by which
we gauge the climb.

    ◦ ◦ ◦ ◦

Three Panels for a Quiet House

I

Here the dawn is slow.
Half a world away
Dawn is a sudden light.
My fingers trace those trees
out on your sleeping back.
You roll across your dream
and find my body hard.
The children wake below.

II

Shut me up with a wish.
It grows as big as my head
inside my head until
I let it out; it grows
into a bear as big
as the cupboard where I am,
and eats me up in a gulp.
I will not tell my wish.

III

Cold metal tastes of breath
and cold water staled
by standing long in the air;
knife, do not touch my mouth.

A knife can cut like grass,
can bend like a willow twig,
can jump up like a fish;
knife, keep from my hand.

⊛　⊛　⊛　⊛

Night before Birth

Tonight the sharp
indefinite edge alerts
each wakeful finger;
houses of the moon
contain wrong planets;
the great bear's a dice
whose bulk imagines
corners on the wind.

Should ridicule
assess the nervous point,
and chart delusion,
we'd see no more far;
the clouds are islands
overcome by beasts;
the bay is scooping
moonlight in both hands.

Sing, cries the Summer,
drunkenly on heat
with draggled finery
of rippling leaves;
but who would risk
the silence between notes
that leant upon this
sweating balcony?

We have a theme,
but so have seas and stars.
So has the Summer
burbling in its gloom.
Our harmony's at odds;
a lover's shirt
shines dankly in the dusk
and giggles come

like bubbles up
the side of this stiff house
whose mobile stars
have horoscopes to spill.
The islands roar,

though dimly, and the chill
foams of the bay
spell messages. It seems

we cannot read them yet.
We have no names
for near arrivals,
gravid but at odds
with plenitude:
the edge of time alerts
but does not solve
the linking of our hands.

   ◉   ◉   ◉   ◉

The Beginning

First Light : the mouth begins
to taste itself and lick
misshapen breath alive;
the eyes are wet with fur;
slowly claws recede
and forests dwindle; scent
abandons cunning; hands
are hands at human sheets.

Gradual muscles harden.
Redness hits the sun.
Down in the sudden bushes
owl and badger sleep
their intricate small dawn
as summer bares its flanks.
The earth is baked to crack.
Trout rot in the stream.

These swollen-bellied days
the sky is empty, drained
of passion and intent;
the flies are idle words
half-heard and half-dismissed;

you move out from our bed,
distended belly taut,
and wade across the room.

You move into the day,
a woman shouldering sea,
your eyes the brown collapse
of seaweed upon rock,
your buttocks ruined hills,
your limbs colossus; now
creation is its tide
and you will have it turn.

You stand at open door
and call the waters down.
The leaves turn in the wind.
The grass begins to shake.
The sea lies very still.
You spit upon a stone
and make the spiders run.
Air tightens in my throat.

The waters gather, gather.
Behind my face the beast
sleeps aftermaths of dark
that you may hear the dream
and make the tidal turn.
You eat the meat I give.
Air trembles to embrace
the final, human cry.

      ● ● ● ●

The Dog in the Night Time

There is no dog.
The night's a crumpled sheet
winking and grinning
to time's jut and heave.
Here in the broken garden
my mouth is dry.

Were there folk at home
I'd have no problems –
the choked intelligible scream,
the hands
lumpy with knuckles, shaking,
the familiar
rasp of threat in my throat –
but no-one's there,
and nothing even to steal,
no locks, no dog.

And the night sweats, wrestling,
gasps hot gusts
between the moist boughs,
thickening what's to come
in clumsy terrors of release.
Grass shakes.
Dangerously, I creak open
the futile door
to flatter vacancy with caution,
roll
the wobbling ball of torchlight
along walls
that stretch then crumple it
on corners braced
against absurdity
to deaden echoes,

and am trapped, ridiculous.
The night
beyond me shudders, stiffens,
holds back till
dams can't but break;
I pause to hear it come
and in the mirror
on the landing see
the two hot eyes,
the watchful snarling fangs.

⊙　⊙　⊙　⊙

At Walden Pond

I stamp on the ice of a man a hundred years dead.
It holds. A pickerel fisherman draws blood
up from black water. Gingerly enough
I step out on the ice, my muscles stiff,
my world precarious as my reasons, and
in each one of my hands a child's gloved hand.

Memory should instruct us here. Ringed barks
of birch-clumps alternate their white with black,
their bronze with silver in crisp parchment rolls.
My daughter slithers, stumbles, almost falls,
but doesn't cry. It's I that almost cry,
lumbered with children under this death-grey sky
a mile from Concord where the war began
and snowdrifts clog the bridge. They seem so young
to risk the ice, though it's more like to hold
their weight than my bear's tread. They can afford
the gestures I can't make, run far, and slide;
slowly we near the shore and the farther wood.

Memory strikes. I remember a school, a master
who soft-shoed this way after lights-out. Order
broke under his footfall. Stamps and jeers
surrounded him. I re-explore the cause.
Whose hunger, and whose guilt? The school was cold.
We hunted him like dogs through the blinding world.

Was that "Vox Populi" or "Demonstration"?
Disorder asks replacement by a name.
Armoured and starved, fish take a naked hook
and leap up to their death. The floorboards shook
in the red-walled dining room. The war
was novel still, and supper cocoa fumed
thin ardours to boy nostrils. He was blamed
as Emperors are blamed, or Governors, pitched
quivering upon anathema. I lurch.
My children scream half-laughters at the risk.

But I don't laugh. His heavy jewish face
blurred as a double image in the glass
of travelling windows has returned to chill
more than remembrance, and the running school
is suddenly upon the ice, a herd
stampeding through the failing light, some dead,
some twisted, from a war they didn't start
and couldn't end. . . . I taste a dull cold hate
heading for Concord and far trees, my hands
held fast by children. Brooding, the hunter bends
above his lines. Red walls blur round the past,
and carefully we cross the darkening pond.

⊛   ⊛   ⊛   ⊛

A Bad Day through the Berkshires

For John and Priscilla Hicks

A bad day; the kids jabbing
screams at my nerves; the Mohawk trail
slowly unwound, past curtaining ice
on flanking rock-slabs
through leaf-brown cleaved hills.
A bad day: time left me
alone there under a dull sky
clicking my shutter;
the car, hauled
to a green standstill by the bridge,
waited.   I clicked.   *Keep this,*
the camera commanded.   *Keep this.*

Things are important.   Rocks, trees,
foams of water.   A man's eye
watches, records.   A woman holds
children warm as the snow piles
higher, higher.   I fear death.
A stone shakes in the stream's flow.

I stand on a stone and teeter, crazy
to make my picture.   Foam spills
foam at my feet.   Clouds herd
clouds round the November sun.
And colour dies.   A dark shutter
remains dark in my nerveless hand.

Pioneer Valley.   Call it the journal
of yet another day lost out
to an obsession. The kids cry
for games and candies. My wife sees
a leafless tree with yellow apples
crowding the twigs.
Should I take that?

The sky's too grey.   The tree stands
close to buildings.   Wires track
from pole to pole across the twigs,
civilized beyond all hope.
My son sees cows.   He likes cows.
When we reach Williamstown we eat.

A bad day. The kids ate,
messily, nothing.   In white rooms
Degas, Renoir.   Perfected flesh.
My daughter, heavy on my shoulders,
calls a naked bather *Mum,*
likes a bronze horse.   I hump symbols
among symbols, my dark eye
dark in the bad light.
                         Evening falls
like a man from a bridge in slow motion
on all our screens in all our homes.

  ⊙   ⊙   ⊙   ⊙

Tiger, Tiger

Sleep's grown a killer;
jungle fills my eyes;
sweat is a skin for the night,
a viscous clad.
Turn me over, boot;
there is blood from my ear:
slack and heavy, I
lie heavy and slack.

My daughter, leaden-eyed
in her night-dress, wanders
down the stairs from her nightmare.
It is still
four o'clock in the morning.
The house is a box.
Voices rattle like dice.
Is our number up?

I once could challenge her night,
but my snarl is dry.
Someone has measured my length
and examined my skin.
The gun butt at my nape
is a wooden god.
I pull myself upstairs
like a sack of rags,

mouthing what dead things mouth:
Be easy, happy!
Uncle is very well.
We are all very well.
Mother sends you her love.
Be happy, easy!
I think I am losing contact. . . .
She falls asleep.

And back below the trees
it is hotter, darker.
If I could stretch one claw
I could scratch a stone's
pelt of wet moss,
tatter the mark of my name
so that a month would pass
before it was gone,

but my claw can't stretch.
It is nearly time
for the knife to open me up,
for the skin to be slit
away from the weight of muscle.
The baby cries,
a kite in the high, mad sky.
More kites. More cries.

And the earth beneath me heaves.
My wife is rising.
When the kites cries end
and the baby is fed,
I am plundered to deafness,
only the slide
and clatter of beaks,
the random noises of feeding

nibbling at total darkness.
Here is here
the solid and the abyss,
the real and the dread.
What was the cause of my name?
Has the blood remembrance?
Heavy and slack, I lie
with glass for eyes.

* * * *

The Voices

I. Voice on a Birthday

"Call me ancient.
I have years for teeth
and gnaw the mountains.
Every road's my spoor
and every town my droppings.
Keep me tracked.
I go to earth before a
stable door.

I have no strategy
but shame. This earth
cannot protect me
or disguise my smell,
even distracts me
with those kills whose bones
are trampled in the mud
about the stall.

Yet here for seconds
once I knelt, close-curled,
unraked by hungers,
and here wish to die
if man can dig me out
or find a way
to dowse the cruel
planet in the sky."

II. Voice of a Witness

"I am what you suppose.
Your truthful eye
hunches me over a cradle,
rewards my trend
with pathways up the hillside,
bleeds my mouth,
shakes the ridiculous
bladder in my hand.

You are never wrong.
Remember this
when I come crawling up the
final stair,
my rags untouchable,
or when I stand
like armour at the deathcell's
opening door.

I am the thing you see,
no other thing.
Do not mistrust the vision
you inform,
or for one second
listen to my voice
as if it were not vibrant
in your own."

III. Voice from a Locked Room

"I kept alone.
I used my other hand.
It populated everything
with light
that glared my eyeballs blind.
It pinned red silk
upon the tyrant Justice
of a thought.

I used my head.
It opened in my hand.
The pomegranate world
spat silver seed
from beauty like a lung
that throbbed to death.
I laid the crying
pities on my bed.

I swore my word.
It listened in my hand,
then rose in judgement
to stand tall and dumb

before the doorway.
No-one yet has knocked.
When will the merciful
Avenger come?"

IV. Voice from a Confessional

"I am destruction
built as a machine.
Whatever engines are,
they tear their springs
and shudder into climax
of dropped steel
sheared through the holding
bolts that lock their frames.

Unction I ask
that dribbles loose as weed
down burnished axles,
triggering their shafts'
enormous wandering,
isolated in
strength unrelated to
my proper task.

I have no product but
my self that wears
out rhythms of its
dislocating drive
to end stock-still, belts broken,
looking out
upon the land
it hungered to believe."

V. Voice of a Finalist

"At last I have self-destruction.
I have removed,
piece by piece, each part of
my whole body,

have finally, in an act of
ultimate logic,
emptied my bag of seed on the
road in spit.
Nothing whole remains.
I walk my shadow
carefully round corners
in case the sun,
trapped by a church or
tenement, refuses
even the semblance that
with twisting hands
plays animals upon the
walls or knits
endlessly cats cradles
for lost children."

VI. Instructions

"Trust me.
I am the god,
the hassock beneath the tree,
the pyx in the rock-pool.
                        Never
is one word I will say.

Kiss me.
I am the bride,
the heat in the seashore lace,
the breast in the whirlwind.
                        Try
that new way to embrace.

Fear me.
I am the man,
the hangman in the egg,
the guard in the teardrop.
                        Push me
over the edge."

    ◎   ◎   ◎   ◎

A Game of Marbles

Rattling the loose marbles around your head,
blood-alleys get like diamonds,
pocked and chipped
until, bled white,
they shatter light with deaths
our playgrounds never missed –
    the death by shame,
    the death by ordeal,
    and the death by lie.

      What do they call you? Patchy Dolly.
      Where were you born? In the cow's horn.

So it has always been.
There have been uncles
blind with starlight
chinking their bottles home,
and chiselled unpronounceables
granted flowers
in tin urns upon particular birthdays.
Even madness,
sliming the raw mouth-corner,
letting the fingers wobble,
always shared
the cellarage with spiders,
and the words
we overheard
spilled innocence in rubble.

      Where were you born? In the cow's horn.
      Where were you bred? In the cow's head.

Like the rest of us, you were uncovered
only when the beast fell down and broke
the marrow out.
That cornucopia brought
us forth in plenty
of good time to learn
another breeding.
Manners starched our throats.
We handled knives like wafers,

spoke our speech
to metronomes of Please,
and Walked, Not Ran.

The old cow, she is dead.

We sucked her bones
on lonely Sundays hunched above The Book
gory with Illustrations in a parlour
tasselled with embarrassments and black
slipperiness of horsehair scrubbing thighs.
I envied goosegirls their green shirts of nettles
and the saints their burns.

Where were you bred?

In the skull of the beast.

The beast is dead.

What's your name?
Puddin Tame.
Ask me again.

Afternoon and evening come quite easy
after that awful morning,
though disturbed
sometimes by the human-headed birds
and sometimes by the phantoms in the fire
that burns, burns, burns
the chips of dung, the blue
soft folding robes of smoke swathed round a prayer
of men hunched under thorn trees by a rock
worn warm and smooth as marbles.

Marbles spin

the planets' wide ellipses out upon
the school charts of infinity.

You roll

the marbles still
on scuffling knees until
the earth diminishes
and playgrounds cry,

Where were you bred? In the cow's head.
Where will you die? In the cow's eye.

⊙ ⊙ ⊙ ⊙

A Slice of Lemon

For Bonamy Dobrée

A slice of lemon in my tea,
a sun
made by the pale crayon in the drawing book
whose colours outrun uniforms,
whose smiles
extend beyond the faces of their rhymes:

there colours spill out; scribbled
free and red,
the mouth escapes the face as if it knew
the passion to transgress,
or how to fit
its clownishness to every passing kiss,

like kissing metals on a black
wet road
the hollow hour between breath and breath
when nothing makes its pass;
at three o'clock
the phone: crashed head-on and a total loss.

At Belle Fourche, South Dakota,
the huge hearse
took us from the automobile graveyard
down to the wide street's haze;
"Hell of a hearse,"
the man said in the back, "No Goddam ash-trays! "

A slice of lemon in my cup,
a moon
slit from the sour round of those moral tales
that brought rags riches;
foolishness is dead,
red silks of blood under November hedges.

A slice of lemon souring up
the mouth;
her skin was greasy and coarse, her jawbone long,
her lipstick the wrong tone;
amendment died
in the dust-clogged grass of a badly cambered lane.

"Hell of a hearse," the man said
at Belle Fourche,
"No Goddam ash-trays," fingering the velvet,
the dusty ebony, the brass.
We drove
along Fifth Avenue on one of those

surrendered empty mornings when
the sun
is lemon yellow, shadows sharp and long,
and memory unvexed as the sky;
it seemed
if we had anything we had the time....

A tartness on the mouth,
a yellow sun,
a lemon yellow moon, spin in her cup
whose eyes are blind as fur,
whose blood has run
dark through the stiffening dusts to which we turn

in time, from time. "Hell of a hearse,"
he said.
We rode Fifth Avenue to the store, and felt
like Lazarus. We lived,
whoever died.
I pin this on her leaden coverlid.

   ◎ ◎ ◎ ◎

Bread

Off Massawa
the ship's ventilation failed.
It was hot as hell.
The assistant baker
pummelled dough till swagging dropsical bellies
flopped and slapped like seals.
He wasn't well,
had prickly heat like red ants crawling up
his hide from heel to neck.
Red-eyed, he swore,
This fucking War!
His girl was a five pound trick
on Lime Street, Liverpool, and all night shift
he bragged about the good times that he'd left.

Bread maddened us.
Unloading the deep oven
scorched skin to a desert.
Wrapped in sacks,
our hands played chuck and grab with loaves whose crusts
could cut us open.
Sweating cobs, we rapped
the black tins empty, clattered them in stacks,
and juggled, cursing, with the hissing loaves.

Five hundred bloody mouths!
the chief spat, hitching
up his gross white belly, fold on fold,
above another mix.
He weighed four hundred
pounds or more, and had a piglike eye.
His number three kept cheerful,
listed brothels
he could vouch for.
None of us could breathe

that hot night off Massawa.
Bread smells good
by loaves, but not by hundredweights.
We raved
by morning, kept

our eyes away from knives
to miss how cleanly the soft firmness sliced
and tore when we tugged free damp parcels that
rose into plumpness sensual as the girls
we fingered every night,
rehearsing vice
on verbal rosaries, all words the same,
till dawn broke more heat out
and we lay slack
and flaccid as the bread
we'd never bake.

    ● ● ● ●

Ghost Shirts

Wovoka believed
in a Messiah,
a newcomer,
the plains black
with buffalo,
taught the tribes to dance,
tell the truth,
not fear death,
and gave them shirts.
This morning shirts
arrive for me
from a dead poet.

Imagination
evolves deaths.
They sang through bullets,
boys in rain
catching the wet in their
mouths, licking
their bare arms.
The shirt fits;
the same shoulders,
the same neck:
I stare out from
his photograph.

The consequences
of prophecy matter
less than the act.
At Wounded Knee
that Christmas time
two hundred died;
for thirty days
the Ghost Dance War
choked up the trails.
The Gods allow
us transformations
the earth foils.

I wear a dead poet's
shirt. Belief
derides the ring of
firelit faces,
as all history;
in Nevada
the prophet,
every victory won,
praised as I praise
the dead that dance
.the dance, are truthful,
and consume.

● ● ● ●

Keep Moving

Keep Moving!
        Somewhere, out of the dark, a voice,
a raggety shuffle, a slump of backs, a dank
sour smell of uniforms.
        I can't guess what
formidable warped memory has blocked
itself out from my mind yet left the voice.
Keep Moving!
        Something lumbers in distress
through foregrounds filled with bodies. Is it food?

114

Fresh clothing? Papers? There's a little space
of itch upon the rough back of my hand
that cries for scratching. Something fills my nose
with – is it dust? Or smoke?
                              Move! I said Move!
I strain my ears to hear the usual joke
and muffled curse that would prove boredom ease,
but somehow someone's fallen on his knees
just at the edge of vision: is he drunk?
The head in front of me is shaven, blank,
and wobbles stupidly. We must be sick.
This memory isn't mine. The needle's stuck
in someone else's groove and won't go on.
Keep Moving There! Keep Moving!
                              Something's gone
away from thinking; some cog doesn't click
and mesh productively; my tongue feels big:
it would be nightmare if the tired sag
of shoulders weren't a comfort, ruling out
enquiry as an effort beyond hope.

It would be nightmare, but it isn't fact
as nightmare is; it doesn't think escape
or consequence; it simply moves, exact
in clumsiness and ignorance, a shape
too gross for comprehension.
                              I am here
a moving lump in space, in time, no more.
I keep on moving. Something tells me *Move!*
Slowly the mass is swallowed by the door.

⊙ ⊙ ⊙ ⊙

The Inscription

The dead girl
wrote to the
poet when she was
alive

and he was
alive and gave him
her poems that
lie

here on the
shelf now he is
dead and her
dead

voice saying
thank you is
no one talking to
no one

❋ ❋ ❋ ❋

History

i. m. J.F.K.

I am a monster.
Among small
crouching years,
I take up

Death in my hand
and Death shakes
wild as a shrew.
I pile bones

high by the wall.
I eat graves.
Chanting,
they bring me
graves to eat.

❋ ❋ ❋ ❋

Remembering Esquimalt

*For Frank Fryett, who, after several years in
a Japanese Prisoner of War Camp near
Nagasaki, was repatriated to a Rehabilitation
Centre at Esquimalt on Vancouver Island*

For rehabilitation
his camp was Esquimalt.
I remembered the kelp
in the tangling sea,
and the English gardens;
he remembered snow,
and eating meat, and
walking alone at night,

those years ago. V. J. Day
he'd seen a mirror.
"Christ," he said, "I'm
bent as a bloody crone! "
"You've had that crook back
all the bloody time
we've been in the mine! " they said:
he hadn't known.

And marching through Nagasaki,
"It looked like a flower
among the stones," he said,
"a cup and saucer
melted and hardened back
into folds of petals.
Lovely it was," he said,
"but I felt sick

thinking about it after."
We drank to Esquimalt,
all that clean blue air.
"One day," he said,
"on the ship from Java
we saw a tanker struck,
and the bastards burning and
running about like mad

ants, all burning whether
they jumped or not.
The sea was on fire," he said.
"We laughed and clapped
and cheered and stamped
to see the buggers trapped.
It isn't nice to think of
the way you get,

or even some things you've seen.
I liked Esquimalt.
They asked us to dances."
He picked up his stick.
"A bit like a rose," he said,
"I should have kept it.
That was one of the things
I should have kept."

    ☆   ☆   ☆   ☆

The Reliquary

To Herbert Siebner

Our fathers were both Artillerymen,
both at Ypres.
Defeated, you were a prisoner,
and I the same
in my victorious desert.
In the still of the evening
we drink beer together.
I show you the box from home.

These are mutual relics:
glass from a shattered
chapel your father's guns
and mine both scored;
even this shrapnel,
bronze rust of a twisted leaf
fallen in Mametz Wood
could have been shared.

118

My father kept everything;
we too have kept
somewhere among our nightmares
a childhood bond:
your German voice is that of a
fear grown friendly;
you are astonished that I am,
you say, "kind";

but, living on this island,
we drink together
in the still of the evening,
the box at our feet.
This half-burned wood
was part of a riotous victory
conflagration:
my father plucked it out.

There are notes in the box.
In the saps at Ypres
the rats ran away with our candles . . .
I picked a stone
from the rubble of San Pierre Church
as a memento . . .
pocketed a plug . . .
cut a chip from a beam. . . .

Ruin is our familiar.
To him it was strange.
Suddenly darkened by memories,
our minds veer
back to cities of fire,
a house unfolding
outward, suddenly peeling
itself to the core.

Nothing is ever forgotten.
We haunt the ghosts
we pack in boxes.
Here's a chunk of iron
the shape and size of my thumb
and marked *A piece*
that very nearly got me.
I wasn't born

the day this burned and
whistled past his ear
to split a sandbag;
nor were you; we both
derive from luck,
victim or seed of iron,
tricks of trajectory,
random errors of death,

a fortunate generation. . . .
You fill your glass
to yarns of a nightmare journey
across a moor,
the thin-jawed captain
watchful for retreat,
the unseen English
creeping round like fire;

and then the hospital train
torn up like cardboard,
the Russian nurse assigning
death or death
with one glance at your motions:
you clown your terrors,
laughing; we laugh
till we are out of breath

at such absurdities.
And yet today
headlines recur:
a Senator has declared
himself against "*The Left*,"
and rapturous crowds
have roared at his talk of "*The Enemy*."
This we endured

before, and have not forgotten
the shapes of death,
the trumpet note cut off high,
the wreaths black-green
against the scrubbed white stone,
the acres of crosses
planted where mankind died
for a song, a name,

a folly, a habit, a God. . . .
Our fathers crawled
the mud we crawled, and heard,
like us, the claim
of Truth for slaughter:
in this cardboard shrine
cold iron, burned wood, dead names
all weigh the same.

◦   ◦   ◦   ◦

Night Poem, Vancouver Island

I

The wind's in the west tonight,
heavy with tidal sound;
the hush and rattle of trees,
the indrawn breath of the shore,
do what they must; waves slap
at the tip and stagger of stones,
and the night tonight is black;
blackness without intent
moves over the globe
as waters move. The shoals
are nosing into the storm.

Blackness moves over the globe.
Will this wind never drop?
The house, awash with air,
swings into the dark,
and, all its lamps ablaze,
challenges time and fear.
I see a wall of ice.
Newspapers fall like flowers.

Turn in the bed, my Love.
Reach out. We almost touch
but, swimmers pulled apart
by arbitrary tides,
are swept out on the night.
Somewhere a hand will find
that delicacy of bone
locked in a glacial year.
We label history now.
Fossils, our smiles extend
the frontiers of the past.
Our kisses breed new terms.

The sea speaks as it must.
We lie together in
a hollow of the sound,
clasped hands entangling bones.
We have our prayers to say.
We have our seed to spend.
We half believe in day.

Sleep is difficult now.
Loudly the pump of the heart
and the rasp of sheet on sheet
answer voice with voice.
Turn in the bed, my Love.
We were a distant tribe
that died. These waters move
the history from our bones.

II

Darkness begins and ends
all that we have and are;
stilled in this night of gale
on the long death of a bed
I reconstruct such lives.
I hear the forest birds
scream over the shore.
I watch the slide of light.
Does history begin?
Feet beat upon bare earth.
Whales rise in the sea.

Something created here:
logic travelled moss
upon the hospitable boles
and lichen dribbled song
from boughs the bines make laws.
Walking to rules of boughs,
listening to wings in the pulse
and breakers over the heart,
I become stone. I pause
to accept the tread of the sun
and the worm under my cold.
Clay is part of me. Grass
patterns me; meshed in rain
by grass, I stare like a toad.
Prayers rot on me like fern.

Do not touch me. Look,
but do not touch. My smile
has red meat in its teeth.
My skin is soft with fur,
and I am wiser than dogs.
Your mouth upon my mouth,
your freed persuasive breasts
could end a different tale
but are irrelevant here.
Press close. Your V of hairs
and buttery mandible nip
most freedoms in the bud,
and your haunches ride
the nightmare to its knees,
but I am not the night,
or free, or beast, or king.
I have no dark or bed.

Light slid up to the shore
here from the stiff sea.
Trees were huge with rain
and the square teeth of bears.
Eagles reach their wings
out above whales; head down,
a toad stood on the lip
of speech and sang its flies.

I am afraid. The hunter
only obeys the laws
of chastity and death.
I do not know his code
that changes as herds grow
or lessen, hungers change.
The salmon leap up through
the membrane. Narrowing hills
shudder, contract, and grip
all they can get. The gun
is levelled, the bow drawn.
Time has its lives to eat.

III

Abandon me. I am lost
in the sweat of my own dark.
Rivers include my eyes.
Forests evolve my hands.
Over the valley hawks
gather into the eye,
watching the movements of death.
I am a name for the sea.

Leave me. Let me be.
Somewhere the ships turn home,
the animals bless the sun,
the thundering lungs fall still,
and the stone eyes smile.
Something created me
because of that one place.
I wear it round my bones.

Who is a wooden mask
painted with teeth. I stood
alone on the island for days
until a whale spoke out.
Its eye was a bead of blood,
its fin curved as an adze,
and its head a hill.
Who is an ivory jaw,
a black glistening skin,
a boat floating alone.

How is a scar on a rib.
I have forgotten craft
and practice. Knives obey
orders I cannot give,
having no rules or words.
Fish come to my hand.
How is a crooked bone,
a bird dropped on the wing.

Why is not my business.
Causes are different worlds.

    I am the sound you make.
Leaf, twig and stone
compose me like a song.
I am the inch you crawl
closer, lifting the bow.
I am the lens of air
through which the hunted move.
We are creation's kind.
Look out! An eagle falls
in every seed we spit.
Fish jump in every thumb.
We are destruction's kin.
Be still. A heron soars
in each astonished breath.

    IV

    Something created here
the lives time has to eat.
Something invented time,
a wrinkle upon the sea.

    Only the dead awake.
The living have no need.
Lapped in a fold of water
travelled across the globe
to end up finally here,
I lift up my arms,
but not to Death. I kneel
but not to Love. I hold
existence close, not beast,
or god, or man, but breath,
more simple and less sure.

Come now, if you wish.
The wind from the west has stilled.
Your mouth upon my mouth
solves nothing but is good.
Light rises from the sea
and time spreads with the light.
Put your body to mine;
we are the world we caused.

❀　❀　❀　❀

Acknowledgements

"Child," "Man with a Guitar," "Advice from the Interior Self," "Flowers and Jar," "Heron," "The Toad," "The Top," and "The Dark Encounter," were included in *Patmos and Other Poems* (London: Routledge & Kegan Paul, 1955).

"The Fence," "The Cat," "The Need," "The Cotton Dress," "The Climb," "Theme," "The Slickensides," "The Horses," "The Exploration," "The Shore," "The Ball," "The Net," "King and Queen," "Third Day Lucky," and "At Tutankhamen's Tomb, Thinking of Yeats," were included in *Third Day Lucky* (London & New York: Oxford University Press, 1958).

"The God," "At the Cavern's Mouth," "Words in a Column," "The Arrival," "A Ballad of Johnnie Question," "A Ballad of Despair," "John Arthur," "The Street," "Sancreed," "Begging the Dialect," "An Uncertain Meaning," "Message for My Father," "Cat and Bird," "Ballad of a Mine and Ballad of the Four Fishers," were included in *Begging the Dialect: Poems and Ballads* (London & New York: Oxford University Press, 1960).

"As I Remember It," "Ancestors," "Joe Sampson," "Angel," "The Brig," "Nothing of Beauty," "Alison Jane Skelton," "A piece of Orange Peel," and "Poem on His Thirty-Fifth Birthday," were included in *The Dark Window* (London & New York: Oxford University Press, 1962).

"A First Ballad of the Muse" and "A Second Ballad of the Muse" were published in *Two Ballads of the Muse* (Cambridge: Rampant Lions Press, 1960).

"Transport Café Crossword" first appeared in *Ambit*. "Quaternion for the Muse" appeared first, in a different form, in *The London Magazine*. "On the Eve of All Hallows" was first printed in *Sage*. The middle section of "Two Moralities and a Footnote" first appeared in *The London Magazine*. "City Varieties, Leeds, 1963," "Remembering Esquimalt," and "Night Before Birth" first appeared in *Poetry Northwest*. "Three Panels for a Quiet House," "A Bad Day Through the Berkshires," and "Tiger, Tiger," were first printed in *Choice* (Chicago). "The Reliquary" and "Bread" were first published by *The Quarterly Review of Literature*. "Ghost Shirts" first appeared in *Prism International*. "Night Poem, Vancouver Island" and "A Game of Marbles" appeared first in *The Massachusetts Review*. "The Voices" was first published in *Poetry* (Chicago).

"A Slice of Lemon" first appeared in *Of Books and Humankind: Essays and Poems presented to Bonamy Dobrée*, edited by John Butt (London: Routledge & Kegan Paul, 1964). "History" first appeared in *Of Poetry and Power: Poems Occasioned by the Presidency and Death of John F. Kennedy*, edited by Erwin A. Glikes and Paul Schwaber (New York: Basic Books, 1964). "Ballad of Billy Barker" was first published as a pamphlet by the Morriss Printing Company, Victoria, British Columbia, in 1965.

I am grateful to the editors and publishers concerned for permission to reprint these poems.